New Directions for Institutional Research

Robert K. Toutkoushian
EDITOR-IN-CHIEF

J. Fredericks Volkwein
ASSOCIATE EDITOR

Using Financial and Personnel Data in a Changing World for Institutional Research

Nicolas A. Valcik

EDITOR

Number 140 • Winter 2008
Jossey-Bass
San Francisco

USING FINANCIAL AND PERSONNEL DATA IN A CHANGING WORLD FOR
INSTITUTIONAL RESEARCH
Nicolas A. Valcik (ed.)
New Directions for Institutional Research, no. 140
Robert K. Toutkoushian, Editor-in-Chief

NEW DIRECTIONS FOR INSTITUTIONAL RESEARCH (ISSN 0271-0579, electronic
ISSN 1536-075X) is part of The Jossey-Bass Higher and Adult Education
Series and is published quarterly by Wiley Subscription Services, Inc., A
Wiley Company, at Jossey-Bass, 989 Market Street, San Francisco, California 94103-1741 (publication number USPS 098-830). Periodicals
Postage Paid at San Francisco, California, and at additional mailing
offices. POSTMASTER: Send address changes to New Directions for Institutional Research, Jossey-Bass, 989 Market Street, San Francisco, California 94103-1741.

SUBSCRIPTIONS cost $100 for individuals and $249 for institutions, agencies, and libraries in the United States. See order form at end of book.

EDITORIAL CORRESPONDENCE should be sent to Robert K. Toutkoushian,
Educational Leadership and Policy Studies, Education 4220, 201 N. Rose
Ave., Indiana University, Bloomington, IN 47405.

New Directions for Institutional Research is indexed in CIJE: Current
Index to Journals in Education (ERIC), Contents Pages in Education (T&F),
and Current Abstracts (EBSCO).

Microfilm copies of issues and chapters are available in 16mm and 35mm,
as well as microfiche in 105mm, through University Microfilms, Inc., 300
North Zeeb Road, Ann Arbor, Michigan 48106-1346.

www.josseybass.com

CONTENTS

EDITOR'S NOTES   1
Nicolas A. Valcik

1. Why Is It Important to Analyze and Use Business and   5
Human Resources Data?
Raymond H. Wallace
This chapter gives the audience a framework of how and why finance
and human resources data are used, as well as the different analyses
that colleges and universities are currently using, to determine institutional operational needs and effectiveness.

2. Using Personnel and Financial Data for Reporting Purposes: 13
What Are the Challenges to Using Such Data Accurately?
Nicolas A. Valcik, Andrea D. Stigdon
This chapter discusses techniques that institutional researchers use to
extract useful data from the human resources and financial information
systems for basic and advanced reports. In addition the chapter discusses how institutional researchers must work with business affairs
areas of operations in order to obtain accurate information.

3. A Beginner's Guide to Integrating Human Resources   25
Faculty Data and Cost Data
Gary D. Levy
Instructional expenses (primarily faculty compensation) account for a
significant percentage of any institution's overall costs or expenses.
Institutional research offices have the potential to enhance institutional
decision making by integrating human resources faculty data and institutional cost data. This chapter outlines issues related to sharing of cost
and human resource faculty data and the institutional researcher's role
in integrating and presenting that data. The first steps in preparing integrated human resources faculty data and cost data are presented.

4. A Four-Step Faculty Compensation Model: From Equity   49
Analysis to Adjustment
Serge Herzog
In today's ever tightening budget for higher education institutions, it is
important for senior administrators to have reliable and accurate data
on the current value of faculty for compensation purposes. If an institution fails to compensate faculty members competitively and equitably,
they will likely seek employment with another institution or an entity
in the private sector. If an institution overpays its faculty members, the
budget used for compensation may very well deplete institutional
resources in other areas. This chapter offers a four-step process to identify possible inequities in faculty compensation and ways to implement
salary adjustments to ensure fair financial rewards and market standards within the institution.

5. Formula Funding, the Delaware Study, and the University   65
of North Carolina
Sarah D. Carrigan
The state of North Carolina uses formula funding as a portion of the
budgeting process for the institutions in The University of North Carolina System. In this chapter, the author will discuss the state funding
model and its relationship to and foundation on the Delaware Study.
Given the central weight that the Delaware Study has on revenue projections across the system, UNC-Greensboro has developed a number
of Delaware Study-related reports, used by the provost and academic
deans for both instructional deployment needs and revenue allocation.
The author illustrates several of these reports.

6. Budgeting for the Kentucky Educational Excellence   79
Scholarship
Melvin E. Letteer
The state of Kentucky uses a very complex model to determine budgetary needs of financial aid for Kentucky high school graduates going
to higher education institutions. This chapter discusses how the Kentucky Higher Education Assistance Authority forecasts future financial
aid requirements for students in the State of Kentucky.

7. Using Return on Investment Models of Programs and   93
Faculty for Strategic Planning
Lawrence J. Redlinger, Nicolas A. Valcik
The state of Texas currently uses formula funding to calculate state
appropriations for public higher education institutions. This chapter
discusses the methodology that The University of Texas at Dallas uses
to analyze what programs are earning for revenue versus what the costs
are for operating each program from state funds.

8. The Role Institutional Research Plays in Navigating the   109
Current Economic Uncertainty
Mary Beth Worley
This final chapter reviews the previous chapters in relation to the current economic situation that universities and colleges are facing across
the country. The author discusses how human resources and business
data, used in the various models and methodologies discussed in this
volume, are impacting the institutional decision-making process.

INDEX   115

EDITOR'S NOTES

No previous *New Directions for Institutional Research* volume has been dedicated to the generalized use of financial and human resource data by institutional researchers. With tightening budgets for higher education and new programs being developed to contend with those shrinking budgets, some institutional research and strategic planning offices increasingly are being asked to provide information on data that are usually under the auspices of business affairs organizations.

Programs such as "The Lean Enterprise Process" (Argent Global Services, 2008) are being implemented at some universities as a way to reduce costs with regard to work processes. In 2008 The University of Texas at Dallas became one of the most recent organizations to implement the Lean Enterprise Process (Jamison, 2008). Implementation of the process at The University of Central Oklahoma has already led the institution to realize cost and personnel efficiencies. Programs such as this require accurate expenditure data to establish a baseline of expenses before program implementation to compare with expenses after implementation (Moore, Nash and Henderson, 2007).

Universities and colleges derive their funding from multiple sources and through various methods. For private institutions, tuition, fees, and alumni giving (and in some cases, research contracts and grants) are the primary sources of income. Private institutions must therefore determine the cost of educating students and set tuition and fees so that those costs are properly financed. Public institutions are partially subsidized by public funds so that tuition and fees can remain low. However, public institutions can be influenced by political models for funding. Hellriegel and Slocum (2007) noted:

> The political model describes decision making by individuals, groups, or units when the parties perceive that they have separate and different interests, goals, and values. Preferences based on self-interest goals may not change as new information is learned. Problem definition, data search and collection, information exchange, and evaluation criteria are methods used to bias the outcome in favor on the individual, group, or unit [p. 375].

Simply stated, legislators pass funding and revenue bills to make their constituents happy. Pfeffer (1992) notes, "Political leaders, too, confirm that the willingness to build and wield power is a prerequisite for success in public life" (p. 13). Therefore public institutions that are receiving revenue from

federal, state, or local entities will put more priority on determining revenue streams that are coming into the public institution (due to enrollment growth) since tuition and fees are set by legislative statutes in many cases.

The fact that public higher education institutions can be heavily dependent on state legislatures for funding does not necessarily indicate that actual costs and expenditures are being taken into account when legislative statutes are being formulated or passed (see Chapter Six for an example of this type of funding). According to Gortner, Mahler, and Nicholson (1987), "Above all else, governmental policies are developed for political purposes. The process by which policies come about and the interests they promote or maintain (whether broad public interest, organized groups, elected or appointed officials, or even bureaus and their members) are political in nature" (p. 35).

Figure 1.1 illustrates the relationship between tuition and fees revenue and state appropriations at various higher education institutions. When combining only two revenue sources for an institution (state appropriations and tuition and fees), one would expect to see private institutions primarily supported by tuition and fees revenue and public institutions supported primarily by state appropriations (other forms of revenue, such as contracts and grants, alumni donations, and endowment assets, are not included in this study). The figure demonstrates this relationship effectively with Har-

Figure 1.1. Proportion of Revenue Derived from State Appropriations Compared to Tuition and Fees, Fiscal Year 2005–2006

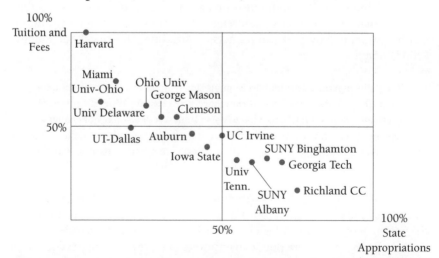

Note: Only tuition and fees and state appropriations revenues included. All other revenue sources are excluded.

Source: L. Redlinger, professor and executive director for the office of strategic planning and analysis at The University of Texas. I extend my thanks to Lawrence Redlinger for producing this figure.

NEW DIRECTIONS FOR INSTITUTIONAL RESEARCH • DOI: 10.1002/ir

vard University on one end of the spectrum (0 percent from state appropriations) and Richland College, an associate-level institution in the Dallas County Community College District, on the other end (84 percent from state appropriations). All other institutions in the figure are public doctoral-granting institutions. The proportion of tuition and fee support to state appropriations runs the entire spectrum from modestly subsidized by the state (Miami University–Oxford, University of Delaware) to heavily supported (State University of New York institutions). This clearly demonstrates how state appropriation revenue streams vary significantly among public institutions due to a multitude of factors, such as elections, legislative agendas, and the local or regional economy, and highlights the potential impact of unexpected legislative changes to the appropriations revenues of some universities.

This volume of *New Directions for Institutional Research* investigates how institutional research offices can analyze financial and human resource data to complete mandatory federal and state reporting and provide timely, quantifiable data for forecasting, planning, and policymaking to decision makers. While the research that uses human resource data can be (and sometimes is) conducted by budget offices or human resource departments, those departments can lack the resources or skills necessary to integrate multiple data sources to produce meaningful analyses and forecasts. An institutional research department can achieve a better understanding of how its institution operates holistically by tapping into human resource data. Furthermore, successful integration of human resource, student, financial, and even facility data can result in more comprehensive reports, which enable upper administrators to make data-driven decisions on institutional policies.

In addition, this volume is designed to address more generalized human resource issues and gradually segue to more theoretical, analytical, and financial uses of human resource data. Chapters One through Four explain why the use of human resource and financial data is important and how these data can be used to address general operational issues. Chapter One discusses the usefulness and practicality of using human resource data as well as general concepts regarding revenue streams that flow into institutions. Chapter Two explores the potential uses for human resource data and the organizational aspects of obtaining such data successfully. Chapter Three examines the integration of faculty, human resource, and financial data to enhance the decision-making process at an institution. Chapter Four addresses the use of human resource data to analyze salary compensation to determine if possible inequities exist in relation to faculty positions and, if so, where salary adjustments can be made.

Chapters Five through Eight relate to formula funding, legislative budgeting mandates, and revenue generation by institutional employees. Chapter Five discusses how formula funding is calculated by the state of North Carolina with the Delaware Study, a cost model the state legislature uses to determine educational funding. Chapter Six reviews the state of Kentucky budgetary process, which combines political decision making and enrollment forecasting to establish financial aid for Kentucky high school students who matriculate in Kentucky's higher education institutions. As a contrast to the funding methodology described in Chapter Six, Chapter Seven describes a method that relies on a mathematical formula to calculate a return on investment from faculty salary data and formula funding generation. Chapter Eight summarizes the volume and discusses formula funding issues and other potential uses for human resource data. These chapters are designed to provide institutional researchers with a broad understanding of how human resource data can be put to greater operational and analytical use and to offer insight into how revenue streams flow through (and are determined by) various organizations across the country.

I thank all of the chapter authors and support staff who worked diligently on this volume. Without skilled and professional institutional researchers to undertake such endeavors, information that could be useful to other institutional researchers and government agencies would not be readily available to provide a foundation for future research and an opportunity to resolve current organizational needs.

Nicolas A. Valcik
Editor

References

Argent Global Services. "The Lean Enterprise Process." 2008. Retrieved Sept. 1, 2008, from http://www.argentglobal.com/Site/Solutions/LeanandSixSigma/tabid/74/Default.aspx.
Gortner, H., Mahler, J., and Nicholson, J. *Organizational Theory: A Public Perspective.* Chicago: Dorsey Press, 1987.
Hellriegel, D., and Slocum Jr., J. *Organizational Behavior: Eleventh Edition.* Mason, Ohio: Thomson South-Western, 2007.
Jamison, C. "From Leadership to LEAN: Transforming UT Dallas." Unpublished report, Business Affairs, University of Texas at Dallas, 2008.
Moore, M., Nash, M., and Henderson, K. "Becoming a Lean University." 2007. Retrieved Sept. 4, 2008, from http://www.sacubo.org/sacubo_resources/best_practices_files/2005_files/UniversityCentralOklahoma-becoming-lean.pdf.
Pfeffer, J. *Managing with Power: Politics and Influence in Organizations.* Boston: Harvard Business School Press, 1992.

NICOLAS A. VALCIK *is the associate director for the Office of Strategic Planning and Analysis and an assistant clinical professor for the Program of Public Affairs at the University of Texas at Dallas.*

1

This chapter provides a framework of how and why human resource data are used, as well as the different analyses that college and universities are currently using, to determine institutional operational needs and effectiveness.

Why Is It Important to Analyze and Use Business and Human Resources Data?

Raymond H. Wallace

In his book *The World Is Flat: A Brief History of the Twenty-First Century*, Thomas Friedman (2005) describes how several "world-flattening" events are causing huge changes in the rate of globalization. Political events such as the fall of the Berlin Wall and technological advances such as the development of the Internet, Web browsers, Web uploading technologies, and data mining technologies have converged to amplify the rate and efficiency with which individuals can create, share, upload, and disseminate ideas and information. A key consequence of this trend is the explosion of innovative ways to communicate more information faster than ever before. These changes have had, and will continue to have, an impact on higher education. Faculty can more readily share information regarding research so that growth to the body of knowledge is advanced at a more efficient and effective pace than in the past.

Not only are we seeing changes in how work is done in higher education, but also in where it is being done. Distance or technology-delivered education, which delivers courses and entire programs to students who are not necessarily on campus, continues to grow (Carnevale, 2006; Foster and Carnevale, 2007). Even college employees may be located in off-campus locations. For example, the institutional research office at Washington State University employs a data warehouse report writer who participates in weekly working meetings with other staff from multiple campuses of the university system. This employee is in fact residing in the Caribbean while

NEW DIRECTIONS FOR INSTITUTIONAL RESEARCH, no. 140, Winter 2008 © Wiley Periodicals, Inc.
Published online in Wiley InterScience (www.interscience.wiley.com) • DOI: 10.1002/ir.266

interacting with staff members from the university system. There are many positions like this throughout colleges and universities that can be performed effectively from off-campus locations. Collaboration software allows employees to have real-time meetings with people from different campuses of a multicampus system, involving audio, video, and desktop-sharing software. The availability of software that allows collaborative work is often free or comes preinstalled on computers. This is what is meant by "world flattening." Anyone can have access to these tools. A university or corporate budget is not needed to make collaborative work possible.

Along with the evolution of information exchange and management, higher education is seeing growing expectations from the government and the general public for increased accountability. U.S. Secretary of Education Margaret Spelling's Commission on Higher Education produced a report outlining problems facing higher education (U.S. Department of Education, 2006). The report states, "Postsecondary education institutions should measure and report meaningful student learning outcomes" (p. 23). Accreditation agencies are called on to increase the public accountability of colleges and universities by providing evidence of performance outcomes. Student learning outcomes is one area that accrediting agencies are emphasizing as they change the way they assess institutions. Accreditors increasingly expect colleges and universities to show evidence of the quality of education provided to students. For example, the Southern Association of Colleges and Schools (2008) requires that an institution write a quality enhancement plan as part of the reaccreditation process that "focuses on learning outcomes and/or the environment supporting student learning and accomplishing the mission of the institution." Understanding what faculty do and how to document their effectiveness in delivering learning outcomes is critical to improved accountability. Colleges and universities need to be able to understand and document the return on the efforts of their faculty.

Another important trend for higher education is that the composition of the faculty and staff of colleges and universities will change rapidly in the coming decade. More than 40 percent of the labor force—64 million baby boomers—may retire by 2010 (Hignite, 2006). This statistic indicates that our society is headed for a reduction in the pool from which colleges and universities can draw employees. Recruiting enough younger faculty and staff to replace the large numbers of retiring baby boomers will be a challenge. The leadership and experience of the retiring cohorts will be replaced by younger employees who have different perceptions of the world, particularly in regard to technology. Decision makers must be able to maximize their use of human resource data in order to manage this transition successfully.

The flattening world, growing expectations of accountability, and retiring baby boomers are just a few of the issues in the rapidly changing work environment that make it essential for colleges and universities to understand a wider variety of business affairs data in order to be competitive and effective. To meet these challenges, institutional research professionals must continually expand their responsibilities and revisit the types of data used and the way that data are managed and applied. The ability to process data more rapidly and decision makers' thirst for data are driving this expansion. It makes sense that simpler routine tasks should be automated to leave more time and resources to add value by transforming data into useful information. In order to inform decision makers of institutional effectiveness, institutional researchers are looking closer at the types of data that have been largely ignored in the past. An example is the analysis of facilities data. Watt (2007) explains how institutions can benefit from better understanding facilities data on classroom management, personnel management, research activity, and return on investment analyses.

Another area of study (and the focus of this volume) into which institutional researchers' roles are expanding is the analysis of human resource and finance data. The following chapters address how institutional researchers can use these data in new ways to add value to their institutions. To accurately analyze data, we need a basic understanding of human resource data structures and the ability to identify the data sources that are best suited for a specific purpose. Our profession must also have an appreciation of the level of productivity of employees and a clear understanding of what is produced. What is the return on investment of instructional faculty? How can we control costs? How are faculty compensated? These are the questions addressed in this volume.

In Chapter Two, Nicolas Valcik and Andrea Stigdon discuss the challenges of dealing with financial and personnel data and the difficulties with data access and extracting information from central data stores. They articulate the importance of institutional researchers' knowledge of business processes in relation to personnel and finance data in order to interpret the meaning of data accurately. In addition, common reports and surveys that involve personnel and financial data are summarized.

It is important to understand the relationship between various campus employees and the institution's data: the people who enter the data (for example, administrative assistants or office managers), the people who maintain the data (including information technology personnel or programmers), and the people who use the data across the institution (such as institutional researchers or budget and planning officers). Data integrity will improve if each of these data handlers has an understanding of the needs of those others. Valcik and Stigdon also examine data security and privacy issues for employees and offer several strategies for dealing with obsolete data systems. Finally, they present solutions for selecting appropriate data sources for a particular analysis, for example, when it would be more useful to use payroll data versus budget data when reporting employee salaries.

Gary Levy gives an overview of cost data concepts in Chapter Three. He explores cost objects and functions and the different ways cost data can be reported. He also identifies a key challenge facing users of faculty-related data: definitional issues. It can be difficult to arrive at common definitions for faculty across institutions. Thanks to surveys such as the Integrated Postsecondary Education Data System (IPEDS) Staff and Faculty Salary surveys, some commonality has been found for defining faculty. However, use of the term *faculty* and the duties associated with it vary by institution. For example, an athletics coach can be a faculty member and never teach a class. Should that person be included in a measure of the faculty-to-student ratio? Universities are also challenged by limited data availability. Some important data elements on faculty, such as faculty productivity and performance data, are not commonly collected and stored in human resource systems. These would be valuable data elements, especially when used in conjunction with cost data.

Occasionally there are data access challenges for institutional research professionals because of technology limitations and the culture of the institution. Organizational politics can often affect whether institutional researchers obtain access to data they need. Levy clearly outlines people's roles at an institution—specifically the roles of data custodian, data trustee, data steward, and data end user—and their different responsibilities for managing and using the institution's data. Levy refers to a data access policy statement at the University of Arizona: "The value of data as an institutional resource is increased and its accuracy improved through its widespread and appropriate use; its value is diminished through misuse, misinterpretation, or unnecessary restrictions to its access."

An Internet search on a portion of the policy's exact wording found several higher education institutions with almost the same policy verbatim. If data access is a problem for the institutional research professionals at a given institution, a conversation with data custodians, stewards, and trustees about adopting this type of policy could help to change cultural barriers regarding access.

Finally, integrating faculty and cost data can be done at a variety of levels, from deans and vice presidents to department units. Often, compiling ratios of cost and faculty data can be useful indicators for an institution. For example, Levy describes such measures as direct instructional expenditures per tenured or tenure-track faculty full time equivalent and scorecard measures that integrate faculty and cost data.

In Chapter Four, Serge Herzog describes in detail an approach that could be used for performing a faculty salary equity analysis. Herzog proposes a four-step process for conducting the statistical analysis. Step 1 uses canonical correlation to identify bias from potential sources of discrimination such as age, gender, and ethnicity/race in faculty pay. Findings from this process determine the inclusion or exclusion of these personal characteristics variables in the final step. Step 2 uses logistic regression to identify and control for bias in tenure promotion. The results from the model can be used to analyze whether a tenure-track faculty member is predicted to be tenured. Misclassifications of faculty members where tenure is predicted but not attained are then scrutinized. Third, multinomial logistic regression is used in a similar fashion to step 2, except that instead of using the binary dependent variable of "tenured/not tenured," a multinomial variable that predicts faculty rank is used. Finally, multiple linear regression determines areas where possible inequity in salary may exist. Factors that are brought into the multiple regression could include market factors such as national salary comparators, measures of career progression, and any personal characteristics determined significant in the initial canonical correlation analysis. Herzog intends this process to help formulate a compensation analysis to examine both internal equity and external calibration in faculty salary.

Sarah Carrigan describes in Chapter Five methods of using data from the National Study of Instructional Costs and Productivity, commonly called the Delaware Study, as an administrative tool for decision makers at the department, college, campus, and system office levels. In North Carolina, the state mandates that each institution in the state system participate in the annual Delaware Study. The University of North Carolina (UNC) system's funding model uses the Delaware Study's information as a basis for externally tested costs. The state system uses this information for both incremental budgets and performance contracts and uses data on faculty workload and instructional costs as benchmarks for the schools. Internally UNC–Greensboro uses the Delaware Study data to assess the extent to which colleges or schools meet institutional priorities and identify programs within units that may be overloaded. It also uses data at the department level for program review.

Using a matrix of the change in student credits and credits per faculty full-time equivalent, Carrigan demonstrates a method for determining the number of faculty positions required to teach for a given discipline category, where categories are determined by the benchmarks produced by the cost per credit hour by discipline and Carnegie classification from the Delaware Study. In addition, enrollment patterns, credit hour production, and student full-time equivalents are projected to allow the institution to forecast tuition revenue. The provost can assess how programs are performing based on historical data and peer norms and allocate funding accordingly.

In Chapter Six, Melvin Letteer discusses the Kentucky Educational Excellence Scholarship program, which uses revenue from the Kentucky lottery to fund scholarships based on high school grade point average (GPA) and ACT score. The Kentucky Higher Education Assistance Authority uses a formula based on GPA and ACT to determine the amount of each scholarship. For every year of high school that a student achieves a GPA of 2.50 and above, he or she earns dollars toward each year of postsecondary education. ACT scores of 15 and above also earn additional money. A database keeps track of each student's earned awards throughout high school. The database then tracks the distribution of awards directly to the postsecondary institution. Each educational institution shares student enrollment data to confirm student eligibility. Letteer closes the chapter by describing how forecasting is done to determine budget projections and award amounts.

NEW DIRECTIONS FOR INSTITUTIONAL RESEARCH • DOI: 10.1002/ir

Return on investment analysis often meets with criticisms in the academic world. However, tight state budgets or inadequate endowments may not allow colleges and universities the luxury of ignoring these issues. Higher education must strategically plan how to focus resources in order to be competitive in the higher education marketplace. Chapter Seven by Lawrence Redlinger and Nicolas Valcik provides a model to answer some of the following policy questions: What is an appropriate level of compensation for a departmental chair? What is an appropriate teaching load? What merit rewards should be available for those who teach large numbers of students and do it well? Why do programs that have similar size and needs have differing costs?

Redlinger and Valcik focus on return on investment for strategic planning purposes. Their model identifies sources of revenue streams through formula funding and tuition and follows those revenues to faculty instructional activity and ultimately to the students who pay the tuition. This cyclical process includes weighted costs per credit hour with respect to student level, the course level, and course discipline, such as science or engineering. The result is a system that focuses on determining the revenue production of each course and allows analysis of return on investment at different levels of aggregation. For example, the return on investment for each faculty member can be couched in terms of surplus or deficit of revenues versus costs. At this level, other factors may come into play, such as special assignments of the faculty member, student evaluations of the faculty member, time of course offering, and grants and contracts. Overall, the system allows college and university planners to estimate revenue generated and determine costs and focus these on specific areas of concern.

In chapter eight, Mary Beth Worley outlines the importance of using business and human resources data in terms of navigating economic uncertainty. Worley discusses the need for institutional researchers to have timely access to accurate and meaningful data sources in order to produce the consequential analyses discussed in the chapters of this volume. The concept of "institutional data" is also discussed in terms of how institutional data policies can have a huge impact on the usefulness of data. Outdated policies, possibly due to political posturing within an institution, can limit the value of an institution's data by not allowing the integrated knowledge and feedback necessary for affective planning and policy discussions.

This volume covers a wide variety of topics related to human resource data and financial data, from the technical aspects of data handling and access to high-level analysis of complex data. The chapters have something for institutional researchers, academics, and administrators at all levels of experience and skills. Chapter Three, for example, may appeal more to readers who are new to the field even as it addresses issues that can reinforce the knowledge of experienced institutional researchers, whereas Chapter Four deals with complex methodologies on faculty compensation that may require an extensive background in statistics. The volume blends theoretical and applied uses for institutional researchers to reference and use within their organization and provides a framework for the increased use of financial and human resource data in institutional research.

References

Carnevale, D., "Online Education Continues to Grow, Report Says." *Chronicle of Higher Education,* Nov. 24, 2006. Retrieved Apr. 30, 2008, from http://chronicle.com/weekly/v53/i14/14a03603.htm.

Foster, A., and Carnevale, D. "Distance Education Goes Public." *Chronicle of Higher Education,* April 27, 2007. Retrieved Apr. 30, 2008, from http://chronicle.com/weekly/v53/i34/34a04901.htm.

Friedman, T. *The World Is Flat: A Brief History of the Twenty-First Century.* New York: Farrar, Straus and Giroux, 2005.

Hignite, K. "The Strategic Importance of Human Resources." *HR Horizons, 1,* 1. 2006. Retrieved Apr. 30, 2008, from http://hrhorizons.nacubo.org/x32.xml.

Southern Association of Colleges and Schools. "Principles of Accreditation: Foundations for Quality Enhancement." 2008. Retrieved Apr. 30, 2008, from http://www.sacscoc.org/principles.asp.

U.S. Department of Education. *A Test of Leadership: Charting the Future of U.S. Higher Education.* Washington, D.C.: U.S. Department of Education, 2006.

Watt, C. "Indirect Costs and Other Uses of Facilities Data at Institutions." In N. Valcik (ed.), *Space: The Final Frontier for Institutional Research.* New Directions for Institutional Research, no. 135. San Francisco: Jossey-Bass, 2007.

RAYMOND H. WALLACE is an administrative planning specialist at Washington State University.

2

This chapter illustrates how institutional researchers can extract useful data from the human resource and financial information systems for basic and advanced reports.

Using Personnel and Financial Data for Reporting Purposes: What Are the Challenges to Using Such Data Accurately?

Nicolas A. Valcik, Andrea D. Stigdon

Although institutional researchers devote a great deal of time mining and using student data to fulfill mandatory federal and state reports and analyze institutional effectiveness, financial and personnel information is also necessary for such endeavors. This chapter discusses the challenges that arise from extracting data from administrative systems, negotiating the administrative process that manages these data, addressing compliance issues, and avoiding common pitfalls while working with personnel and financial data.

Reports That Use Personnel and Financial Data

Although most mandatory reports and institutional effectiveness issues involve student metrics, a number of reports and analyses require financial and personnel data. The National Center for Education Statistics (NCES) at the U.S. Department of Education is the foremost agency, followed by regional accreditation agencies such as the Southern Association of Colleges and Schools (SACS), that relies on financial and personnel data from institutions. NCES reports from its Integrated Postsecondary Education Data System (IPEDS) surveys that focus on financial or personnel data include fall semester staff, finance, employees by assigned position, salaries, and student

financial aid. Regional accreditation agencies demonstrate a great deal of disparity in what they require of their member institutions. SACS is perhaps the most rigorous of the regional accreditation firms. It requires colleges and universities to submit substantial financial documentation to demonstrate the institution's solvency and stability. According to SACS (2008), an institution must send documents pertaining to its recent financial history to prove financial stability; financial profile information and other measures of financial health; audits of financial aid programs; documents indicating that the institution exercises appropriate control over all its financial resources, as well as externally funded or sponsored research and all its physical resources; information that shows the institution takes reasonable steps to provide a healthy, safe, and secure campus environment; and data demonstrating that the institution properly operates and maintains physical facilities.

Many public colleges and universities must also report financial and human resource information to state boards. In Texas, for example, the Texas Higher Education Coordinating Board requires a faculty report (CBM008) for all personnel with faculty rank or those who engaged in instruction as part of their assignment. This report must include demographic information such as gender, ethnicity, and date of birth, as well as salary by source type and tenure information. This information can be provided only by human resource and payroll or budget databases. The facility inventory report, which is completed every fall semester, is linked to the course scheduling report (CBM005) to verify an institution's space use rate and, through the space projection model, determine its current and future facility needs.

In addition to federal, state, and regional entities, there are major national studies, such as by the National Science Foundation, that also require financial data from institutions. Two surveys managed by the National Science Foundation are the Research Facilities Survey and the National Survey of Graduates and Post-Doctoral Students. The Research Facilities Survey is heavily dependent on facilities information, requiring participating institutions to report square footage devoted to research, condition of facilities, designation of research space to specific fields of study, monies expended or committed toward renovations and repairs, monies budgeted for major renovations and new construction, and information technology resources. In addition to student head counts by gender, ethnicity, and full- or part-time status, the National Survey of Graduates and Post-Doctoral Students requires information on mechanisms of support for graduate students and personnel information in postdoctoral fellows and research scientists. Obtaining this information requires having access to contracts and grants databases for grant sponsor information, payroll systems to determine which students might be supported through stipends or campus work other than graduate assistantships, and human resource databases for information on personnel classified as postdoctoral fellows and nonfaculty research scientists.

Other surveys require human resource or budget system information, such as those by the College and University Personnel Association and the

American Association of University Professors. For institutional research purposes, especially for effective benchmarking and assessment of graduate program effectiveness, salary data on graduate assistants and faculty can be essential for maintaining or improving an institution's ability to compete with other universities for the best faculty and most lucrative federal grants. Additional uses of these data include the Student and Exchange Visitor Information System tracking, producing studies on international scholars, and even the construction of mailing lists for public relations events such as the president's annual holiday party held for faculty and staff.

Organizational Theory and the Administrative Process: Working with Subcultures

Universities are complex organizations "oriented to the pursuit of relatively specific goals and exhibiting relatively highly formalized social structures" (Scott, 1987, p. 22). The various subcultures within a university—academic departments with their attendant faculty and support staff, and administrative components of managers, office staff and information technology personnel—share a common environment in which the primary goals of the institution are the effective provision of research, teaching, and service. An example of this operational structure can be seen in Figure 2.1.

However, to be effective in their duties, administrative assistants and office managers tend to focus exclusively on the requirements of their

Figure 2.1. One Data System, Two Purposes

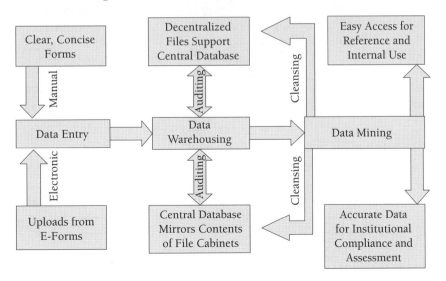

immediate areas. Very few people at this level have the time or wherewithal to ponder more holistic issues, such as how another department might use their area's budget documents to assess institutional effectiveness or whether the way in which the data are recorded and stored might affect how a programmer uses the data. Information technology personnel must concern themselves with the security, integrity, and maintenance of data systems and do not have the time to wonder about how the data will be used. At most, they are concerned with writing a successful program and less with how those data are ultimately used. In other words, "by providing integrated subgoals, stable expectations, required information, necessary facilities, routine-performance programs, and in general a set of constraints within which required decisions can be made, organizations supply these 'givens' to individual participants" (Scott, 1987, p. 48).

Individuals' duties may constrain them into tightly defined roles, such as office support, technology support, and management, but institutional research provides an opportunity for all participants to integrate their knowledge toward organizational assessment and obtain important feedback that can lead to improved administrative processes. Although elements of the administrative process such as timesheets, hiring documentation, and account reconciliations are typically the concern of support staff such as administrative assistants and office managers, familiarization with front-end processes is essential for understanding how personnel and financial data are captured and stored. Table 2.1 refers to the various subcultures in regard to institutional data.

Consequently, the understanding that support staff have for the administrative process is vital to evaluating and comprehending data obtained from human resource systems. This level of understanding is also crucial for effective data cleansing, particularly when the system may include various exceptions to written rules such as dual appointments, partial appointments, special assignments, and common typographical errors. The daily maintenance of personnel records, position controls, and account management thus becomes intertwined with data analysis. Cultivating a working relationship with support staff and familiarizing oneself with the administrative process for one's institution can yield beneficial results. Table 2.2 shows how the different subcultures communicate with each other in regards to data and operational issues.

Key Issues with Mining Financial and Personnel Data

At its most basic level, a university's financial and personnel structure is similar to that of any private company: people are hired to perform work and are provided pay and benefits in return, the university receives revenue and has expenditures, and the university owns real estate and controlled assets that must be tracked and maintained. Unlike private companies, many universities make financial decisions based not on maximizing profits but on the best possible means to provide an educational service while

**Table 2.1. Relationship of University Data to Three
Significant Subcultures**

	Administrative Assistant	Programmer	Institutional Researcher
Primary responsibility	Direct support of academic or administrative unit	Maintenance and security of institution's IT infrastructure	Ensuring compliance with reporting obligations and dissemination of data for assessment and planning
Relationship to data	Entry	Extraction	Analysis
Use of data	Selective	Minimal	Holistic
Access to university systems	Minimal	Complete	Variable
Need for data accuracy	High, but limited to specialized area	Low	High
Data accuracy measured by:	Effectiveness in resolving local needs	Successful execution of program	Passing audits designed to verify logic, consistency, degree of variance from previously reported results

Table 2.2. Questions That Can Enable Subcultures to Interact

Administrative Assistant	Programmer	Institutional Researcher
Why are certain procedures in place?	Why do certain individuals need access to certain systems?	How can I effectively explain to other personnel how these data are used?
How are data I do not need being used by the rest of the institution?	How can I determine if the data I have extracted are accurate?	How can I involve other personnel in the reporting and assessment process so that it becomes meaningful and useful to them?
How do the activities of other personnel affect my data?	How will these data be used? Why are they important?	
Who else uses the data that I need? Do they use my data differently than I do?	Why were the data input inaccurately? Are there controls that can be set to limit erroneous entries?	What challenges do other personnel face when entering or extracting data? How can I assist them with these challenges?
Are there tools that can reduce the time I spend on data entry and minimize data entry errors?		

remaining in compliance with federal and state regulations. Within this environment, subcultures such as the budget office or the human resource office, also owners of significant amounts of data, can shape how the entire university manages its data and thus affect how data can be used. The following issues often arise in such an environment and bear discussion.

FERPA Compliance. The 1974 Family Educational Rights and Privacy Act (FERPA) is a federal law that protects the privacy of student educational records. Generally universities must have written permission from a student prior to releasing any information from a student's educational records. However, FERPA allows universities to disclose those records, without consent, to the following parties or under the following conditions (34 CFR sec. 99.31):

- School officials with legitimate educational interest
- Other schools to which a student is transferring
- Specified officials for audit or evaluation purposes
- Appropriate parties in connection with financial aid to a student
- Organizations conducting certain studies for or on behalf of the school
- Accrediting agencies
- To comply with a judicial order or lawfully issued subpoena
- Appropriate officials in cases of health and safety emergencies
- State and local authorities, within a juvenile system, pursuant to specific state law

Universities may disclose, without consent, "directory" information such as a student's name, address, telephone number, date and place of birth, honors and awards, and dates of attendance. However, universities must tell students about directory information and allow students a reasonable amount of time to request that the institution not disclose directory information about them. It is imperative that all university personnel who have contact with student information be made aware of this law so that data on a student are not inadvertently disclosed in an unlawful fashion.

This issue dovetails with another consideration when handling personnel data: social security number confidentiality. Both the Federal Privacy Act of 1974 and the Social Security Act of 1990 concern the safeguarding and proper use of social security numbers when handling personnel data and when or if to release these data for reporting purposes. In Texas, for example, this is a great concern because the Texas Higher Education Coordinating Board requires the use of social security numbers as identifiers for students and faculty in all state reporting. Employees responsible for the maintenance of records that contain social security numbers are required to observe all institutionally established administrative, technical, and physical safeguards in order to protect the confidentiality of such records. Proper and effective interaction among data entry personnel, data owners, information technology (IT) personnel, and institutional researchers becomes crucial when all parties are required to comply with federal confidentiality laws.

Computer Resources. An institution's computer resources can become a source of irritation and discouragement if the system is difficult to use or is obsolete. As of 2008, The University of Texas at Dallas (UT-Dallas) continued to use a mainframe system that runs the SCT product HRS DB2 and requires the programming language FOCUS to extract information and Job Control Language to direct programs to extract data from the correct production tables. The institutional researchers at UT-Dallas maintain a strong working relationship with the computer operators, information security personnel, and COBOL programmers who work in the university's IT department to assist with accessing DB2 tables, problem solving with programming errors, production library maintenance, backing up data, and providing general assistance or training. Although many other universities simply rely on the IT department to write and execute programs that extract large data files for analysts to manipulate and refine, the institutional researchers at UT-Dallas have discovered that working regularly with IT personnel and learning how to program from the mainframe resulted in a more efficient and expedient data extraction while simultaneously freeing IT personnel to focus on their core responsibilities.

Programming on a mainframe system can provide several challenges, particularly with calendar dates and length of contract. Many universities structure their fiscal year around their academic year, which means that the beginning of the fiscal year usually occurs in fall semester. At UT-Dallas, the fiscal year starts September 1 and ends August 31. All employment contracts, appointment dates, and budget information are structured around September 1 as the first month of the year, or month 01. However, the university must also interact with government agencies, notably the Internal Revenue Service, which considers January the first month of the year. All income tax information and paperwork must follow the calendar year. The calendar year, with January designated as the 01 month, is also part of the computer system's structure. When programming against the human resource or payroll systems, it is necessary to convert the calendar month into the proper code to designate its place in the fiscal year. An example is shown in Table 2.3. This step is essential, particularly when analyzing faculty who have nine-month appointments.

Calculating total salary for hourly employees became a special issue in constructing an extract of data on staff. Most employees in a university are paid a fixed salary rate once per month for a nine- or twelve-month period. This rate is based on a full seven-day week at four weeks per month to ensure that the monthly employee is paid the exact rate each month regardless of month length. Hourly and student employees, however, have variable salaries based on the actual hours worked in a two-week period. Furthermore, the turnover rate with student and hourly employees can be quite high since some employees are seasonal (such as landscaping) and students are affected by their academic workloads and graduation. Hence, an

**Table 2.3. Conversion from Actual Year Months
to Fiscal Year Months**

Month	Fiscal Year Month	Actual Year Month
January	05	01
February	06	02
March	07	03
April	08	04
May	09	05
June	10	06
July	11	07
August	12	08
September	01	09
October	02	10
November	03	11
December	04	12

hourly employee's "contract" might end after one month or three months or five and one-half months. To overcome these issues, a table containing the total days of each month was constructed, including a date variable for February to compensate for leap years (Table 2.4).

The staff extract then used a special wage calculation to normalize hourly rates to monthly rates:

1. Monthly hours worked = Hours worked per week divided by seven days multiplied by the number of days in a month

**Table 2.4. Program Table for Calculating
Number of Days per Month**

Month	Number of Days
January	31
February	&Day (Substitute Variable)
March	31
April	30
May	31
June	30
July	31
August	31
September	30
October	31
November	30
December	31

2. Days worked per year = Length of employment determined by subtract-ing start date (day/month) from end date (day/month)
3. Hourly workers' monthly rate = Days worked multiplied by pay rate multiplied by hours
4. Annual salary = Add total salary earned each month to determine how much an hourly employee earned that year

Since hourly employees work Monday through Friday while monthly employees' pay rates include Saturday and Sunday, the first step in this cal-culation accounts for weekends. Steps 2 and 3 normalize the hourly employees' variable hours over months with variable days so that the resul-tant monthly pay rate is comparable to that of monthly employees. Using this methodology enabled the program to capture the pay rate per month accurately for hourly workers.

Budget File Versus Payroll Data. For many years, institutional researchers at UT-Dallas had to rely on a budget file to analyze and report salary information. Although the budget file is a useful tool for reporting and planning, it has significant limitations. It can be difficult to link budgeted monies to individual student workers or casual laborers because these posi-tions are typically group positions with a pool of money set aside for hiring various individuals. Another limitation is that the budget file does not reflect actual salary paid over the course of a fiscal year. This can hamper forecast-ing efforts and detailed analyses of departmental turnover and expenditures.

Unlike the budget file, which is static, the payroll and human resource systems are quite dynamic. Since the payroll department is directly respon-sible for the disbursement of monthly and semimonthly paychecks, errors can be quickly identified and corrected in the human resource system. Therefore, the data are tightly controlled, highly accurate, and current. For this reason, accessing and using payroll data for institutional analysis became an important goal.

To capture payroll information accurately required several meetings with human resource personnel and the payroll director. Key issues that would require unique programming solutions were immediately identified: employees who were paid from multiple accounts or held dual appoint-ments, employees receiving no monetary compensation, employees receiv-ing stipends and supplemental income, calculation of total pay for hourly and student employees, and programming against a fiscal year that does not correspond to a calendar year.

Dual appointments typically occur when tenured or tenure-track fac-ulty members are also administrators, such as presidents, provosts, depart-ment heads, and deans. This differs from personnel who experience midyear reclassifications, promotions, or transfers because those individuals do not hold two or more assignments simultaneously, as do tenured and tenure-track administrators. Dual appointments can complicate otherwise straight-forward reporting. State reports require tenure status information regardless

NEW DIRECTIONS FOR INSTITUTIONAL RESEARCH • DOI: 10.1002/ir

of whether the employee is engaged in instruction and research is compensated from an academic account, or the person is a full-time administrator compensated from an administrative account. As an example, at our institution, the university president is recorded on the CBM008 faculty report to the Texas Higher Education Coordinating Board even though he is not actively engaged in teaching or conducting research. The president's situation is hardly unique; many other employees with dual appointments, such as the provost, the associate provosts, the deans, and several vice presidents, also find themselves on the state faculty report because they hold tenure and faculty rank. To complicate matters further, dual appointments at UT-Dallas must be recorded in the human resource system in a manner that does not allow the total full-time equivalency to exceed 100 percent. An administrator who holds faculty rank is paid from an administrative account at a 100 percent full-time equivalency, while the faculty appointment is budgeted for a certain salary rate but at 0 percent full-time equivalency. Hence, the same individual can be recorded twice in two areas: as a full-time administrator compensated at an administrative salary rate at 100 percent full-time equivalency and as a tenured faculty member in an academic unit with a faculty salary rate but at 0 percent full-time equivalency.

Complications can also occur when an employee holds one position but is compensated from accounts held by two or more departments. IPEDS staff and faculty reports and National Science Foundation reports require that individual faculty be designated into discrete academic disciplines. An instructor who collaborates in an interdisciplinary program or is assigned to two departments equally must be assigned fully to one discipline to satisfy federal reporting. The instructor's primary departmental assignment is designated by variables in the human resource system that determine their primary assignment.

However, when one is conducting intensive research into institutional effectiveness or faculty return on investment, it is important to be able to capture all monies earned by instructors regardless of account type. A budget file might show the instructor's base salary with his or her primary department, but it might not reflect actual compensation from stipends, supplemental income, or a restricted contract or grant account that pays for this person's salary for a certain percentage of time, for example, during the summer. In contrast, an institution's payroll system will capture all monies paid out to individuals and from which accounts and will update this information on a monthly, not yearly, basis.

Account types become an important factor to consider as well when dealing with personnel information, particularly for state reporting. In Texas, public institutions must report instructor salary as well as percentage of compensation by account type (state, restricted, designated, auxiliary, or overload funds) to the state. For example, a tenured professor might be paid 80 percent from an academic account and 20 percent from a contract or grant account. The original budget file would have temporary account

NEW DIRECTIONS FOR INSTITUTIONAL RESEARCH • DOI: 10.1002/ir

numbers beginning with 9 to denote contract and grant reports, while the payroll system would have the final account number including updated salary information.

The payroll system is of limited use when trying to identify individuals who are not receiving paychecks: faculty who are on leave without pay, volunteers who are not being paid to teach courses, and individuals who teach at an institution but are paid from an external source of funds not processed through the institution's financial system, for example. For state reporting purposes, faculty on leave of absence for sabbaticals must be identified. The staff extract developed by the Office of Strategic Planning and Analysis at UT-Dallas, for example, excludes all salary lines with 0 percent full-time equivalency with the exception of stipends that have a specific code. This removes duplicate entries for administrators who hold faculty rank, staff who are on leave of absence, and retirees. Unfortunately, it also eliminates faculty on sabbaticals or other leaves of absence. Instructors on leave of absence are reported by the various academic departments to the registrar's office and the provost's office, which manually input these instructors into the student information system.

The reporting of supplemental pay for faculty is also an important area of concern for institutional research. Public institutions in Texas are required to report faculty stipends and supplemental income to the coordinating board whenever the income is taxable. This additional income must also be properly recorded in the proper account type. By meeting with personnel from the budget office, institutional researchers were able to identify where stipend and supplemental income information was recorded in the system and how this income information could be successfully extracted. At UT-Dallas, stipend and supplemental income information is tied to a special class code. If the class code is equal to a certain value and the full-time equivalency of the account in question is 0 percent, then the pay rate amount is in fact a stipend that is taxable income and must be included on the CBM008 report.

The human resource information system uses job codes to designate different types of active and retired employees. Common job code categories are student worker (both hourly and work-study), retiree, faculty, casual (hourly) laborer, classified staff, and administrative/professional staff, which are all refined into numerous subcategories. Understanding these codes is essential for accurate reporting, particularly because mandatory reports require that some employees, especially retirees, be excluded from final reports. The institution must maintain data on retirees in the human resource system because the institution is responsible for the disbursement of retirement and health benefits. Therefore, understanding which codes correspond to employees who must be excluded is very important.

Former employees are also not immediately removed from the system once their employment is terminated because the record of their employment must be retained at least for the duration of the fiscal year. Attention to employment end dates becomes necessary in identifying former employees.

Conclusion

Numerous mandatory federal and state reports, as well as key studies and surveys, require institutional researchers to use and leverage financial data to supplement student data used for other reporting purposes. Understanding and effectively working with the financial and human resource systems available to the institutional researcher requires cooperation and communication with data owners in payroll, budget, and human resource offices, as well as information security and IT personnel. If institutional researchers do not use human resource or financial data correctly to get information on costs of employees, the resulting forecasts and revenue projections will be incorrect. Recognizing the presence of departmental subcultures that have their own goals and challenges will enable more successful integration of knowledge toward more effective organizational assessment and a more efficient and accurate reporting process. Cooperating with data owners and IT personnel also reveals new ways of extracting information and overcoming obstacles toward achieving data accuracy.

References

Scott, R. *Organizations: Rational, Natural and Open Systems.* (2nd ed.) Upper Saddle River, N.J.: Prentice Hall, 1987.
Southern Association of Colleges and Schools (SACS). *2008 Interim Edition: Principles of Accreditation: Foundation for Quality Enhancement.* Decatur, Ga.: Southern Association of Colleges and Schools, 2008.

NICOLAS A. VALCIK *is the associate director for the Office of Strategic Planning and Analysis and an assistant clinical professor for the Program of Public Affairs at The University of Texas at Dallas.*

ANDREA D. STIGDON *is the administrative services officer for the Office of Strategic Planning and Analysis at The University of Texas at Dallas.*

NEW DIRECTIONS FOR INSTITUTIONAL RESEARCH • DOI: 10.1002/ir

3

This chapter presents essentials of human resource faculty data and cost data and how they can be integrated to facilitate institutional decision making.

A Beginner's Guide to Integrating Human Resources Faculty Data and Cost Data

Gary D. Levy

A sage provost once told me that managing institutions of higher education "is all about people and money." Simply put, resources and their distribution are principal performance drivers in most organizations, higher education institutions included. Therefore, it should not be surprising to find a chapter in this volume detailing how institutional researchers can integrate certain human resource faculty data and cost data to inform higher education decision makers about managing academic units such as departments or college and academic institutions as a whole. The mere facts that instructional expenses account for a significant percentage of any institution's overall expenses and that faculty salaries and wages and benefits typically account, on average, for more than 60 percent of most higher education institution's annual expenses make such a discussion practically intuitive (Barr, 2002; Bowen, 1980; Hample, 1980; Middaugh, 2000, 2005).

This chapter serves as a beginner's guide to some essentials of human resource faculty data and cost data and their integration into products to facilitate institutional decision making. It begins with a brief overview of general higher education cost data concepts, followed by a similar synopsis of relevant higher education human resource data. The chapter then outlines issues related to the sharing of cost and human resource faculty data and institutional researchers' roles in integrating and presenting these data and information. Next, the first steps in preparing integrated human resource

NEW DIRECTIONS FOR INSTITUTIONAL RESEARCH, no. 140, Winter 2008   © Wiley Periodicals, Inc.
Published online in Wiley InterScience (www.interscience.wiley.com) • DOI: 10.1002/ir.268

faculty data and cost data and information are presented. Finally, some contemporary applications of integrated human resource faculty data and cost
data are shared.

Many readers have likely heard some version of the adage, "Great
[blank] is/are born, and not learned." As relevant as this saying might be for
teachers or actors, it is not very applicable to institutional researchers.
Although I have no desire to enter into a nature versus nurture debate as it
pertains to institutional researchers, one would be hard-pressed to describe
how skills involved in working in a contemporary institutional research
office (Matier, Sidle, and Hurst, 1995; Sanders, 1999; Volkwein, 1999) could
be linked to some genetic or innate predisposition or skill set. Based on my
personal experience, I believe that institutional researchers are more often
made than born.

That said, I warn all readers that I entered institutional research several
years ago after a lengthy professorial career and was thus made and not
born. This chapter therefore represents observations and experiences from
my varied roles in higher education, combined with aspects of the diverse
literature on cost factors in higher education (Bowen, 1980; Brinkman and
Allen, 1986; Brinkman, 1981; Hample, 1980; Simpson, 1991).

Common Higher Education Cost Data Concepts

Dyke (2000) offered a comprehensive explanation of many of the common
costs, or expenses, within institutions of higher education (see also Barr, 2002;
Milam, 2008). Moreover, the National Association of College and University
Business Officers, the Financial Accounting Standards Board (for private institutions), and the Governmental Accounting Standards Board (for public institutions) have provided standard cost reporting practices for higher
education institutions. Readers who are not institutewide budget officers or
accountants in a higher education setting should refer to a recent Integrated
Postsecondary Education Data System (IPEDS) Finance Survey or an institution's annual financial audit or consolidated financial report and statement
(Barr, 2002; Winston, 2000) to help gain some understanding of general cost
(or expenditure) objects and functions in higher education.

Expenditure or cost objects are essentially categories of costs that label
what certain monies were specifically used for (Armstrong, 2000). These cost
objects might be familiar to institutional research directors who oversee the
budget and spending of their office. Examples include categories such as costs
for utilities (heating, cooling, electricity, and water), repair and maintenance
of buildings, new equipment or perhaps copying, and of course salaries,
wages, and benefits. Each of these objects can also be broken into more discrete units of analysis if necessary: salaries for tenured and tenure-track faculty, salaries for part-time faculty, salaries for postdoctoral students, salaries
for graduate assistants, and so on. In addition, cost objects are often categorized into those for personnel and those for nonpersonnel or operating

expenses (sometimes referred to as "above the line" and "below the line," respectively).

Expenditure or cost functions, as their name implies, inform the reader about what function or purpose for which monies have been spent or are intended to be spent. One common abbreviation that an institutional researcher working with cost data will hear is E&G costs, which refer to education and general expenditures, typically major costs that align with a higher education institution's mission. Some standard cost functions that revolve around aspects of a higher education institution's mission are instruction, research, public service, academic support, auxiliary enterprises, institutional support, libraries, operation and maintenance, student scholarships and fellowships, and student services. Table 3.1 shows a sample table for cost functions by college.

Accordingly the distribution of expenditures across cost functions should in general inform the reader of an institution's mission and primary values (Bowen, 1980; Brinkman, 2000). Similar to cost objects, one may drill down on cost functions to gain insights into more discrete costs. For instance, under the cost function of instruction, one might examine instructional costs

Table 3.1. Sample Table of Cost Functions by College (dollars in thousands)

| | Cost Function | | | | |
Fiscal Year A	Instruction	Research	Public Service	Other[a]	Total
College					
Architecture	$2,511	$272	$64	$49	$2,896
Business	15,184	957	1,651	2,021	19,813
Education	10,904	65	96	1,205	12,270
Engineering	21,583	41,161	1,115	3,936	67,795
Fine Arts	10,319	125	1,026	1,947	13,417
Health	9,699	370	954	1,545	12,568
Humanities	20,748	344	589	2,038	23,719
Law	6,825	7	191	2,660	9,683
Medicine	67,102	102,256	251,702	5,445	426,505
Mines and Earth Sciences	5,701	9,411	1,767	1,611	18,490
Nursing	9,269	1,437	958	189	11,853
Pharmacy	6,028	14,318	6,829	2,002	29,177
Science	30,554	30,202	533	2,028	63,317
Social Behavioral Sciences	17,861	5,056	1,944	1,621	26,482
Social Work	3,414	569	2,580	782	7,345
Total	237,702	206,550	271,999	29,079	745,330
Percentage of total	31.9%	27.7%	36.5%	3.9%	100.0%

[a]Includes academic support, student services, student aid, institutional support, operations and maintenance, and hospital cost functions.

pertaining to general academic offerings versus those for remedial offerings or perhaps versus vocational or technical training offerings, and so on.

Armstrong (2000) noted that it is often useful to build a time series table showing per annum expenses for specific cost functions of an institution or college, such as in Table 3.2. Changes in the total expenses associated with a specific cost function for a particular college from one year to the next may coincide with a change in expectations or activities associated with that function for that college (such as a change in emphasis on teaching versus research). One would hope that such variations would correspond to a priori strategic planning and budgeting rather than simply being post hoc realizations (for example, expansion of some unit's instructional activities or a unit's instructional or research activity after hiring on more faculty the prior year).

Deans and vice presidents should find tables such as these useful in determining how and where to allocate or reallocate future resources, par-

Table 3.2. Selected Cost Functions by College by Fiscal Year (dollars in thousands)

College	Instruction			Research		
	Fiscal Year C	Fiscal Year D	Percentage Change	Fiscal Year C	Fiscal Year D	Percentage Change
Architecture	$2,468	$2,511	1.7%	$234	$272	16.2%
Business	13,179	15,184	15.2	1,253	957	−23.6
Education	9,752	10,904	11.8	94	65	−30.9
Engineering	20,543	21,583	5.1	38,311	41,161	7.4
Fine Arts	10,327	10,319	−0.1	133	125	−6.0
Health	8,869	9,699	9.4	642	370	−42.4
Humanities	19,283	20,748	7.6	365	344	−5.8
Law	6,611	6,825	3.2	8	7	−12.5
Medicine	60,985	67,102	10.0	109,949	102,256	−7.0
Mines and Earth Sciences	4,971	5,701	14.7	9,556	9,411	−1.5
Nursing	7,803	9,269	18.8	2,146	1,437	−33.0
Pharmacy	5,239	6,028	15.1	13,721	14,318	4.4
Science	29,164	30,554	4.8	32,374	30,202	−6.7
Social Behavioral Sciences	18,162	17,861	−1.7	5,607	5,056	−9.8
Social Work	3,358	3,414	1.7	570	569	−0.2
Total	$220,714	$237,702	7.7%	$214,963	$206,550	−3.9%

Source: University of Utah Office of Budget and Institutional Analysis, http://www.obia.utah.edu/budget/expenses/pdf/table4.pdf.

ticularly in association with institutional expectations regarding specific cost functions by college and college activities. Institutions containing a combined budget and institutional research office (an organizational structure that I support) would be likely to create a table like this, as well as tables containing other common revenue sources, such as tuition and fees, auxiliary services, investment income, unrestricted endowment monies, and state appropriations for public institutions.

Overall, expenditure and cost objects and functions are potentially helpful metrics for gaining an understanding of ways that resources are used within an organization or unit. Moreover, examination of a unit's expenditure and cost objects and functions presumably illuminates the priorities or foci of that unit. Changes in the distribution of monies across cost objects and functions over time (typically over fiscal years) help tell a story about changes or stability in a unit's operations and organizational priorities. As I show in this chapter, integrating these types of costs data with other sorts of data (such as faculty data) can help explain the efficiency and operational priorities of a given organizational unit.

Common Types of Higher Education Human Resource Faculty Data

Not surprisingly, the type and quality of data about faculty collected and maintained in higher education institutions vary widely (see Chapter Two, this volume). This is in part likely due to substantial variability in the ways that institutions are organized regarding which offices are responsible for different types of faculty data (including demographic data, salary data, and tenure and promotion history) and to the broad range of higher education institutions as a whole. There are some common types of faculty data that are relatively well identified and defined. Such data are routinely collected by most institutions and can be collapsed or folded into some common and useful categories. These two circumstances are likely attributable in part to some of the reporting requirements of IPEDS surveys concerning faculty.

Although some institutional research offices assist in completion of the IPEDS Human Resources surveys or even complete entire sections or surveys of IPEDS reports including data on faculty, staff, and administrators, it is an institution's human resource office that more commonly completes IPEDS surveys. As such, an overview of the common types and categories of faculty data included in the IPEDS Human Resources surveys is warranted. However, other potentially informative types of faculty data—for instance, faculty productivity or performance data—are less commonly collected by human resource offices or institutional research offices, let alone being combined with cost data to facilitate decision making (see Arreola, 2000).

Many institutional researchers are familiar with the two primary IPEDS surveys that call for faculty data: (1) Fall Staff Survey and (2) Salary, Tenure, and Fringe Benefits of Full-Time Instructional Faculty Survey. Whereas the

Fall Staff Survey is quite comprehensive in its counts of university personnel (including faculty and others), the Salary, Tenure, and Fringe Benefits of Full-Time Instructional Faculty Survey is focused exclusively on full-time instructional faculty.

The slicing and dicing of human resource faculty data for the Salary, Tenure, and Fringe Benefits of Full-Time Instructional Faculty Survey often begins with the identification of faculty considered full-time instructional faculty. The IPEDS definition of instruction is "a functional expense category that includes expenses of the colleges, schools, departments, and other instructional divisions of the institution and expenses for departmental research and public service that are not separately budgeted. This category includes general academic instruction, occupational and vocational instruction, community education, preparatory and adult basic education, and regular, special, and extension sessions. Also includes expenses for both credit and noncredit activities."

In addition, IPEDS defines *faculty* as,

> persons identified by the institution as such and typically those whose initial assignments are made for the purpose of conducting instruction, research or public service as a principal activity (or activities). They may hold academic rank titles of professor, associate professor, assistant professor, instructor, lecturer or the equivalent of any of those academic ranks. Faculty may also include the chancellor/president, provost, vice provosts, deans, directors or the equivalent, as well as associate deans, assistant deans and executive officers of academic departments (chairpersons, heads or the equivalent) if their principal activity is instruction combined with research and/or public service. The designation as "faculty" is separate from the activities to which they may be currently assigned. For example, a newly appointed president of an institution may also be appointed as a faculty member. Graduate, instruction, and research assistants are not included in this category.

Ultimately IPEDS defines full-time instructional faculty as "those members of the instruction/research staff employed full time and whose major regular assignment is instruction, including those with released time for research. Also, includes full-time faculty for whom it is not possible to differentiate between teaching, research and public service because each of these functions is an integral component of his/her regular assignment."

Although the previous IPEDS definitions appear quite comprehensive and specific, institutional researchers have pointed out that often there are substantial differences across institutions in guidelines for classifying faculty in general, and full-time instructional faculty in particular (Gater and Lombardi, 2001; Milam, 2008). Although admittedly frustrating, these definitional differences should not be surprising to institutional researchers given the many types of higher education institutions, their different types of faculty, and their varied organizational structures. For example, some institutions use faculty rank information to categorize faculty as full time and instructional ("regular faculty"), whereas other institutions with more specific and detailed individual job descriptions for faculty use those to determine the percentage of time a faculty member is designated to instruct. Some schools simply use a job title as a means to categorize faculty as instructional versus, say, research faculty. In addition, certain institutions might use a combination of budget, cost, and faculty rank data to designate full-time instructional faculty.

Gater and Lombardi (2001) suggested that the IPEDS Fall Staff Survey may be more precise than the IPEDS Salary survey in terms of providing head counts of institutional faculty. However, once again, variability among institutions in terms of how certain types of positions are categorized as faculty or not (librarians, for example) make cross-institutional comparisons a bit perilous. Nevertheless, the IPEDS Fall Staff Survey probably contains fewer definitional shortcomings and variances than its salary survey cousin. The IPEDS Fall Staff Survey breaks down faculty data as a function of part-time or full-time status, primary function or occupational activity (such as primarily instruction, primarily research, and so on), gender, contract length, academic rank for tenured or tenure-track faculty, salary range, and fringe benefit information.

Data contained in the IPEDS Fall Staff survey are certainly informative and also provide opportunities for comparisons to other institutions using any of several data tools on the National Center for Education Statistics Web site. However, the "row by row" or "detail level" faculty data used to complete the IPEDS Fall Staff Survey combined with relevant cost data are where institutional researchers can help in producing integrated reports to facilitate decision making. Specifically, by integrating cost data with different categories of human resource faculty data, institutional research offices can add value above and beyond simple reporting of cost and faculty data.

Issues in Accessing Cost and Human Resource Faculty Data

Similar to the higher education institutions where they reside, institutional data pertaining to costs and human resources frequently exist in separate organizational areas or silos or in decentralized and discrete information technology modules (Nelson, 2005). Consequently the requisite steps needed to gain access to these distinct data sources need to be configured prior to any institutional research office being able to combine and integrate an institution's human resource faculty data and cost data. Unfortunately, it has been my experience that arrangements regarding data access across silos or domains are often difficult to negotiate.

Decentralized storage and maintenance of distinct data types was the norm, perhaps by necessity, in the formative years prior to or shortly following the advent of powerful and affordable information technologies. Often in the early days of data crunching, data and (if available) specialized software needed to deal with such data were housed within or close to the organizational unit tasked with generating reports using those data. For us in higher education during this time, data typically appeared on large pieces of engineering graph paper or data cards or magnetic tape. As mainframe computing became more prominent, though, the functional silos of expertise and reporting remained. Data were collected and housed in large mainframe computers, but access to data and computer time and power was limited.

More recently, the development of powerful and inexpensive personal computing hardware and software has changed ways institutional researchers work with institutional data (Sanders, 1999). In addition, the emergence and predominance of enterprise-level relational database systems (including Banner, Datatel, Oracle, PeopleSoft, and Sybase) have dramatically changed the means by which end users, including institutional researchers, can access institutional data. However, many institutions as a whole (and institutional research office in particular) have struggled to move from a mainframe mentality, characterized by rather autocratic and centralized control of access to row-level data, to a more contemporary model where approved end users can work more directly with needed data tables and fields from enterprise system database tables.

Because institutional data now reside within centralized and highly integrated enterprise relational databases, theoretically it should be easier for institutional researchers or an institutional research office to securely access such data. However, it typically is not the information technology that now inhibits, or prohibits, access to institutional data by institutional researchers; it is more often organizational politics and antiquated information technology policies and practices. Unfortunately, many of the hopes and promises regarding ease of data access and reporting that were proffered as enterprise systems spread have not borne fruit.

As Valcik and Stigdon note in Chapter Two in this volume, "an institution's computer resources can become a source of irritation and discouragement if the system is difficult to use or is obsolete." However, it is likely that difficulties regarding access to data have had less to do with limitations in information technologies or systems and more to do with lack of relevant institutional commitments and documented policies regarding data access. Thankfully, admirable, albeit slow, progress is being made in development of data and information management policies within higher education institutions that use enterprise-level relational database systems.

That said, it is imperative that a clear set of explicit policies regarding data access exists prior to allowing institutional research offices to gain access and ultimately integrate human resource faculty data and cost data. A first step in the development of such policies, as they would affect human resources and cost data (or budget or financials data), is an institutional commitment to the notion of institutional data, as well as acceptance of identified data custodians, data trustees, and data stewards for such data.

Institutional researchers, who are typically end users of data and information creators, not data entry entities, are all too familiar with the often-heard comment, "Well, HR owns those data" or "The owner of student data is the registrar." The idea of institutional data contrasts with remarks such as the former and holds that data regarding students, faculty, staff, monies, and so on that are acquired or maintained by an institution's employees in the performance of their assigned jobs are the property of an institution. The notion that an institution, rather than an institutional office or unit or individual person, "owns" data about its students, faculty, staff, budgets, expenditures, endowment, and so on is an essential premise that precedes any establishment of a robust and genuine data and information management policy. Furthermore, end users with a demonstrable need for access to certain types of institutional data (a valid need to know) in the performance of their assigned jobs should have straightforward and relatively simple access to such data. This idea is characterized nicely by the University of Arizona, whose institutional data access policy begins, "The value of data as an institutional resource is increased and its accuracy improved through its widespread and appropriate use; its value is diminished through misuse, misinterpretation, or unnecessary restrictions to its access."

Once the concept of institutional data has been accepted, or at least approved by an institution's senior leadership, the next step is to identify appropriate data custodians, data trustees, and data stewards, as well as their respective roles, authorities, and responsibilities. Data custodians have responsibility for the information technology systems used to create, receive, store, process, or transmit institutional data. Typically data custodians are associated with the information technology organization that houses and oversees an institution's enterprise level database systems. Note that data custodians do not make decisions about data access. However, these custodians often do influence or discern what software applications or hardware may be used to access data that the data steward has determined as legitimate for an end user to access.

Data trustees are typically persons from senior university administration or management who are typically at the vice president, associate or vice provost, dean, or university director level (but not the chief information officer) and have planning or policymaking responsibilities for data in their operational area. For example, the data trustee for student demographic data and student course enrollment data would likely be a provost, senior vice president of academic affairs (the chief academic officer), or perhaps even a vice president of student affairs. The data trustee for expenditure data would commonly be the vice president of administration or vice president of finance. The data trustee for human resource data concerning faculty is often the vice president of human resources or that vice president's direct report.

Data stewards are university officials who have planning and policy-level responsibilities for access and management of institutional data in their functional areas. Appointed by a data trustee to manage a subset of data,

data stewards are responsible for data accuracy, integrity, and privacy. For example, a provost or vice president of academic or student affairs might appoint the registrar as the data steward over data about enrolled students. Similarly, the vice president for finance might appoint the comptroller as the data steward for institutional expenditure or cost data.

What happens in institutions where the notion of institutional data and the accompanying concepts of data trustees, stewards, and custodians have not been embraced or well documented? Anecdotally, many institutional researchers and administrators have experienced this situation to some degree. In the past, end users (including institutional researchers) were essentially stuck with what data they could get. Such situations often led to great amounts of time being spent by decision makers quarreling among whose data were "correct" rather than providing a set of shared data where productive discussions could take place and decisions could be made. However, a troublesome trend has occurred as computer hardware has become less expensive and software has become easier to use. Institutions have experienced a dramatic proliferation of shadow databases and redundant data systems built by end users who are frustrated or disgruntled with their continued unsuccessful attempts to gain access to the institutional data that they need. Besides cost and inefficiencies of such practices, the result for the institution is often decision-making paralysis as different constituencies argue with one another over whose numbers are "right." Seldom are any genuine data-based decisions made under such circumstances.

In summary, the practice of providing integrated cost data and human resource faculty data is a good idea only in theory if practices and policies regarding data access are not established. Institutional researchers, as the primary integrators of university-level institutional data on most campuses, likely need to take leadership or facilitative roles in the establishment of institutional data and information management policies. Familiarity with the concepts of institutional data, data custodian, data steward, data trustee, and end users will come in handy in any attempt to establish such policies.

First Steps in Integrating Human Resource Faculty Data and Cost Data

The previous sections have delineated some of the fundamental types of data on faculty and costs. Specifically, cost data can be organized using aspects of fundamental cost objects or functions, whereas human resource faculty data can be structured around many of the categories of IPEDS data used to complete the Fall Staff Survey. Table 3.3 shows a fairly typical example of a report integrating cost and some human resource faculty data, as well as other types of data.

Table 3.3 can help inform decision making at a variety of levels. For example, deans and vice presidents could use information in this table to

**Table 3.3. Sample Integrated Data Report for a College
or Academic Department**

Fiscal Year K	Cost Function		
Cost Object	Instruction	Research	Public Service
Personnel salaries			
Professionals	$26,509	$0	$0
Faculty (full time)	977,775	0	0
Faculty (part time)	33,968	0	0
Graduate students and assistants	0	5,046	0
Postdoctoral fellows	0	10,321	0
Tuition and scholarships	0	6,122	0
Hourly staff	62,224	0	3,211
Fringe benefits	0	0	0
Total personnel	1,100,476	21,489	$3,211
Nonpersonnel Support			
Miscellaneous wages	3,721	160	0
Travel	9,045	6,645	1,534
Supplies and expenses	18,315	9,420	845
Occupancy and maintenance	1,287	0	0
Equipment	0	0	0
Other expenses	9,083	0	0
Credits and transfers	0	0	0
Travel	0	0	0
Total nonpersonnel	$41,451	$16,225	$2,379

Source: Based on Armstrong (2000).

understand where resources in a given unit (say, a college or academic department) are being expended and focused. Additional information could come from a drill-down time series, such as that presented in Table 3.4 and similar to that of Table 3.3. Here decision makers can quickly see whether greater or fewer resources have been used for personnel versus nonpersonnel expenses over time and, more important, whether distribution of monies across cost functions of instruction versus research has changed over time. Tables such as these inform decision makers as to what entities and activities within a unit are being emphasized or at least being allocated greater resources when placed within the context of an institution's or unit's mission or strategic planning or resource allocation or reallocation. A logical next step would be to examine relationships between expense and resource allocation and some measurable end product of that specific unit, such as student credit hours, number of majors, and number of students, or courses taught.

Middaugh's extensive undertaking with the University of Delaware Study of Instructional Costs and Productivity is a clear example of how

NEW DIRECTIONS FOR INSTITUTIONAL RESEARCH • DOI: 10.1002/ir

Table 3.4. Sample Integrated Data Report for a College or Academic Department

Cost Object	Instruction			Research		
	Fiscal Year S	Fiscal Year T	Fiscal Year U	Fiscal Year S	Fiscal Year T	Fiscal Year U
Personnel salaries						
Professionals	$26,509	$27,039	$27,850	$0	$0	$0
Faculty (full time)	977,775	1,026,664	1,083,130	0	0	0
Faculty (part time)	33,968	34,647	36,726	0	0	0
Graduate students and assistants	0	0	15,000	5,046	5,197	5,353
Postdoctoral fellows	0	0	0	10,321	11,147	11,815
Tuition and scholarships	0	0	0	6,122	6,734	7,206
Hourly staff	62,224	62,500	0	0	0	0
Fringe benefits	0	0	0	0	0	0
Total personnel	1,100,476	1,150,850	1,162,707	21,489	23,078	24,374
Nonpersonnel support						
Miscellaneous wages	3,721	3,907	4,102	160	168	185
Travel	9,045	9,950	10,944	6,645	6,977	7,396
Supplies and expenses	18,315	19,780	21,363	9,420	10,362	11,087
Occupancy and maintenance	1,287	1,326	1,365	0	0	0
Equipment	0	0	15,000	0	0	10,000
Other expenses	9,083	9,750	10,043	0	0	0
Credits and transfers	0	0	0	0	0	0
Total nonpersonnel	$41,451	$44,712	$62,817	$16,225	$17,507	$28,668

Source: Based on Armstrong (2000).

examination of expenses (in this case, direct instructional expenses and instructional cost function and also the number of faculty full-time equivalents) is integrated with varied types of quantifiable end products or output measures, such as student credit hour generation, class sections taught, full-time equivalent, and head count of total students taught (Middaugh, 2000, 2001, 2005; Middaugh, Graham, and Shahid, 2003; Middaugh and Isaacs, 2005; also see Chapter Five, this volume). Essentially the two key ratios of note that the Delaware Study methodology puts forward are, by department, (1) direct instructional expenses per student credit hour (SCH) and (2) direct instructional expenses per full time equivalent (FTE) student. In addition, the ratio of organized class sections per FTE tenured and tenure-track faculty is quite informative as well. (See Chapter Five, this volume, for a fuller description of the Delaware Study methodology.)

Middaugh (2000) provided a helpful list of indicators or end products to inform decision makers, derived in part from the integration of cost data and human resource faculty data. This list of indicators includes degrees awarded, number of majors (enrolled or declared presumably), organized class sections taught by tenure-track versus tenured faculty versus non-tenure-eligible faculty; percentage of student credit hours taught by tenure-track versus tenured faculty versus non-tenure-eligible faculty, and percentage of student credit hours taught by FTE faculty. Of course, greater value is derived when these types of comparisons can be made over time, as is seen in Table 3.5 (borrowed from Middaugh, 2005).

Simple ratios essentially are quotients comprising some quantifiable end product and some cost totals that are mainstays of cost accounting and higher education budget planning (Brown and Gaber, 2002; Minter, 1982; also see Chapter Five, this volume). Notably, Armstrong (2000) suggested that calculating ratios involving costs data divided by some measure of productivity or output allow examination at a "cost per x" level. Armstrong (2000) recommended that useful ratios include direct instructional expenses per student credit hour taught, direct instructional expenses per FTE student taught, and direct research and service expenditures per FTE tenured or tenure-track faculty person.

Middaugh's work has added even greater value by allowing decision makers to benchmark across institutions of similar types and between institutions of differing Carnegie classifications. Such research (see Middaugh, 2001, 2005) has shown significant differences in the cost of producing student credit hours, degrees, and so on as a function of the type of department or discipline (such as electrical engineering versus psychology), type of institution (for example, research-extensive versus comprehensive institution), proportion of faculty who are tenured or tenure track versus non-tenure-eligible, level of instruction (undergraduate versus graduate), and total amount of instruction (including SCH) produced.

However, as useful as some groups of decision makers might find the Delaware Study data to be, my experience suggests that the array of data that

Table 3.5. Direct Instructional Cost per Student Credit Hour Taught: Delaware Study Benchmarks for Comprehensive Colleges and Universities

Department	Fiscal Year F	Fiscal Year G		Fiscal Year H		Fiscal Year I	
	Cost/SCH	Cost/SCH	Percentage Change	Cost/SCH	Percentage Change	Cost/SCH	Percentage Change
Accounting	$169	$176	4.1%	$175	−0.1%	$173	−1.1%
Anthropology	106	132	24.5	110	−16.7	91	−17.3
Biological Sciences	135	149	10.4	162	8.7	154	−4.9
Business Administration	145	144	−0.7	142	−1.4	147	3.5
Chemistry	168	181	7.7	174	−3.9	179	2.9
Communications	134	138	3.0	138	0.0	130	−5.8
Computer Science	135	155	14.8	165	6.5	195	18.2
Economics	112	126	12.5	111	−11.9	124	11.7
Education	185	180	−2.7	188	4.4	184	−2.1
Engineering	339	320	−5.6	358	11.9	383	7.0
English	109	112	2.8	115	2.7	112	−2.6
Financial Management	157	174	10.8	163	−6.3	158	−3.1
Foreign Languages	139	147	5.8	139	−5.4	140	0.7
Geography	121	103	−14.9	118	14.6	118	0.0
Geology	160	144	−10.0	149	3.5	155	4.0
History	99	103	4.0	106	2.9	95	−10.4
Mathematics	105	106	1.0	111	4.7	113	1.8
Nursing	316	318	0.6	326	2.5	310	−4.9
Philosophy	124	118	−4.8	127	7.6	111	−12.6
Physics	165	167	1.2	181	8.4	173	−4.4
Political Science	129	131	1.6	131	0.0	118	−9.9
Sociology	99	100	1.0	105	5.0	103	−1.9
Visual and Performing Arts	174	180	3.4	199	10.6	192	−3.5
Average	$153	$157	3.1%	$161	2.1%	$159	−1.5%

Source: Middaugh (2005).

NEW DIRECTIONS FOR INSTITUTIONAL RESEARCH • DOI: 10.1002/ir

the study provides can be overwhelming or nonintuitive to some end users. In addition, the Delaware data are focused at the level of the department, but often deans and chairs have questions about individual faculty. As such, it is sometimes useful to present varied ratios, similar if not identical to those from the Delaware Study, such as in Exhibit 3.1.

In summary, when the goal is to integrate higher education human resource faculty data and cost data, some good beginning points are to examine standard cost functions along with categories of human resource faculty data used to complete IPEDS Human Resources surveys. Clearly, an institutional research office that is integrated with or frequently works closely with an institutional budget office will find it less difficult to accomplish these types of integrative reports. Institutional research offices may already be familiar with some of the fundamental ways that cost and faculty data might be integrated if their institutions participate in the Delaware Study. Nevertheless, institutional researchers who are beginning to consider generating these types of integrative reports would do well to use simple ratios involving cost and faculty data. Fortunately much groundwork has been completed that can facilitate decisions about what types of ratios might inform decision making within a given higher education institution.

Exhibit 3.1. Some Sample Ratios to Facilitate Decision Making

Direct instructional expense ratios
  Direct instructional expense/Total FTE undergraduate students instructed
  Direct instructional expense/Total FTE graduate students instructed
  Direct instructional expense/Total SCH undergraduate students instructed
  Direct instructional expense/Total SCH graduate students instructed
  Direct instructional expense/Total enrolled undergraduate majors
  Direct instructional expense/Total enrolled graduate majors

SCH and enrolled majors ratios
  Total undergraduate SCH undergraduate instructed/Total FTE faculty
  Total graduate SCH instructed/Total FTE faculty
  Total enrolled undergraduate majors/Total FTE faculty
  Total enrolled graduate majors/Total FTE faculty
  Total undergraduate SCH students instructed/Total FTE part-time and/or non-
    tenure-track faculty
  Total graduate SCH students instructed/Total FTE part-time and/or non-
    tenure-track faculty

Total personnel expense ratios
  Total personnel costs/Direct instructional expenses
  Total personnel costs for tenured/tenure-track faculty/Direct instructional
    expenses
  Total personnel costs/Total enrolled majors (undergraduate)
  Total personnel costs/Total enrolled majors (graduate)

NEW DIRECTIONS FOR INSTITUTIONAL RESEARCH • DOI: 10.1002/ir

Additional Uses of Integrated Human Resources Faculty Data and Cost Data

The many cost ratios, cost functions, cost objects, and human resource faculty data described in previous sections are certainly useful in enhancing decision makers' understanding of resource allocation and productivity at the departmental and college levels. However, what some decision makers often ask for from institutional researchers is a more microscopic analysis focused on smaller units. Fortunately human resource faculty data and certain aspects of cost data can be accessed at these varied levels.

It was with this type of request in mind that departmental and a faculty scorecards were developed. The scorecard notion (Kaplan and Norton, 1996, 2001) is not new, but its use in higher education settings has been somewhat sporadic for various reasons (Birnbaum, 2005). Nevertheless, the scorecard literature (see, for example, Kaplan and Norton, 2001) and personal experience suggest that use of a scorecard methodology including cost data and human resource faculty data might facilitate decision making and assist managers in planning and budgeting.

The departmental scorecard (see the sample in Table 3.6) includes a variety of information relating to costs, instructional activity, and faculty. The faculty scorecard (see the sample in Table 3.7) provides indexes of individual

Table 3.6. Sample Psychology Departmental Scorecard

Departmental Scorecard: Psychology	Fiscal Year X	Fiscal Year Y	Fiscal Year Z
Total FTE faculty	15	13	15
College average	10	11	10
Percentage tenured	33%	38%	33%
College average	65%	65%	65%
Average salary: Professor	$68,240	$70,351	$71,061
$n =$	8	8	8
Percentage of OSU or AAUP average	101%	99%	102%
Average salary: Associate professor	$52,885	$54,520	$55,071
$n =$	3	3	3%
Percentage of OSU or AAUP average	98%	95%	97
Average salary: Assistant professor	$47,346	$48,810	$49,303
$n =$	4	2	4
Percentage of OSU or AAUP average	103%	99%	99%
Direct instructional expenses	$1,852,000	$1,889,040	$1,930,599
College average	$2,458,960	$2,510,598	$2,563,321
Total personnel costs as of direct instructional expenses	95%	96%	96%
College average	97%	97%	97%

(continued)

Table 3.6. (continued)

Departmental Scorecard: Psychology	Fiscal Year X	Fiscal Year Y	Fiscal Year Z
Tenure/tenure track faculty as percentage of total instructional faculty	63%	64%	63%
College average	61%	61%	61%
Instructional Activity: Psychology			
Undergraduate FTE	771	773	771
College average	725	728	725
Graduate FTE	56	58	59
College average	25	26	25
Undergraduate SCH	9,250	9,275	9,255
College average	8,525	8,700	8,565
Graduate SCH	500	525	530
College average	355	360	360
Undergraduate majors	175	182	177
College average	77	85	80
Graduate majors	40	42	44
College average	25	25	26
Ratios: Psychology			
Direct instructional expense/ Total undergraduate FTE instructed	$2,403	$2,444	$2,503
College average	3,392	3,449	3,536
Direct instructional expense/ Total undergraduate SCH instructed	200	204	209
College Average	288	289	299
Direct instructional expense/ Total graduate FTE instructed	33,336	32,384	32,784
College average	98,358	96,561	102,533
Direct instructional expense/ Total graduate SCH instructed	3,704	3,598	3,643
College average	6,927	6,974	7,120
Direct instructional expense/ Total FTE instructed	2,241	2,273	2,326
College average	3,279	3,330	3,418
Direct instructional expense/ Total SCH instructed	190	193	197
College average	277	277	287
Direct instructional expense/ Total enrolled majors	8,614	8,433	8,736
College average	24,107	22,824	24,182

Note: OSU = Oklahoma State University; AAUP = American Association of University Professors.

Source: OSU Faculty Salary Survey Introduction, http://vpaf.okstate.edu/irim/FacultySalary.html. American Association of University Professors, http://www.aaup.org/aaup

Table 3.7. Sample Faculty Scorecard, Department of Psychology

Rank	Academic Year G-H Assistant Professor	Academic Year H-I Assistant Professor	Academic Year I-J Assistant Professor	Academic Year J-K Assistant Professor	Academic Year K-L Associate Professor
Annual salary	$51,500	$52,530	$53,581	$54,652	$60,117
Departmental average for rank	$51,010	$52,540	$54,117	$55,199	$61,500
Percentage of OSU or AAUP average	102%	104%	104%	105%	100%
Annual instructional salary	$51,500	$52,530	$53,581	$35,524	$39,076
Instructional Activity					
Annual course sections taught	4	4	2	4	6
Annual departmental average	4	4	4	4	4
Annual college average	6	6	6	6	6
Annual undergraduate SCH instructed	1,650	1,800	1,050	1,500	900
Annual departmental average	1,500	1,590	1,530	1,530	798
Annual college average	1,590	1,602	1,620	1,530	1,548
Annual graduate SCH instructed	0	0	0	0	66
Annual departmental average	42	60	60	48	48
Annual college average	48	48	54	42	48
Annual undergraduate FTE instructed	138	150	88	125	75
Annual departmental average	125	133	128	128	67
Annual college average	133	134	135	128	129
Annual graduate FTE instructed	0	0	0	0	7
Annual college average	5	5	6	5	5
Annual undergraduate advisees	50	50	50	50	45

Table 3.7. (Continued)

Rank	Academic Year G-H Assistant Professor	Academic Year H-I Assistant Professor	Academic Year I-J Assistant Professor	Academic Year J-K Assistant Professor	Academic Year K-L Associate Professor
Instructional Activity (continued)					
Annual departmental average	45	48	45	45	45
Annual college average	30	31	31	32	33
Annual graduate advisees	0	0	0	2	2
Annual departmental average	4	4	5	4	4
Annual college average	2	2	2	2	2
Ratios					
Annual instructional salary/Undergraduate SCH instructed	$31	$29	$51	$24	$43
Departmental average for rank	$33	$33	$33	$33	$34
Annual instructional salary/Graduate SCH instructed	NA	NA	NA	NA	$911
Departmental average for rank	NA	NA	NA	NA	$985
Annual instructional salary/Undergraduate FTE instructed	$375	$350	$612	$284	$521
Departmental average for rank	$395	$395	$393	$395	$399
Annual instructional salary/Graduate FTE instructed	NA	NA	NA	NA	$5,329
Departmental average for rank	NA	NA	NA	NA	$8,325

Note: Annual instructional salary is an individual's annual salary minus the amount paid for by grants or other fiscal buyouts. OSU = Oklahoma State University; AAUP = American Association of University Professors.

Source: OSU Faculty Salary Survey Introduction, http://vpaf.okstate.edu/irim/FacultySalary.html.

American Association of University Professors, http://www.aaup.org/aaup

performance as well as some departmental and college- or university-level benchmarks as well. Both scorecards contain some similar metrics, as well as relevant benchmarking metrics. In addition, the departmental and faculty scorecards follow nicely from the college-level Delaware study reports and provide helpful means by which to make intracollege (cross departmental) and intradepartmental (cross faculty) comparisons. Again, anecdotal experience has suggested that deans and chairs often find intra-institution comparisons, and ones taken over a three- to four-year time series, to be more helpful in their strategic budgeting activities than higher-level cross-institution benchmarking. The latter type of benchmarking, specifically across peer institutions, has been more useful to vice presidents, regents, and trustee members, however, in gauging institutional performance and framing budgets for the institution or at the college level.

Conclusion

After completing this chapter, the reader should have a basic understanding of some cost objects and functions in higher education institutions, as well as some of the common types and categories of faculty data used to complete IPEDS Human Resources Surveys. Although examination of these data on their own may be informative to decision makers in terms of how an institution or unit is using its financial and human resources, greater value often comes from the integration of these data. The templates and ratios contained in the Delaware Study provide excellent examples of this type of integration for departmental and college analyses. In addition, this chapter suggests some other ways to integrate cost data and human resource faculty data as scorecards to inform decision making that may be more applicable to more microlevels of study.

Presumably one benefit of participation in the Delaware Study is the ability to externally benchmark one's own institution or departments to similar units. However, successful benchmarking (in these cases, external benchmarking) is dependent on the ability to identify suitable peer units and participation of those units' institution in the study. When these two conditions are met, the Delaware Study can yield informative and valuable information for decision makers. Fortunately, in addition to external benchmarking (or when attempts to benchmark externally are not successful), the examination of ratios and integrated cost and faculty data in time series, and at the more microlevels of scorecards, may also be of value for decision making.

Finally, whereas normative methods for comparing units are often very worthwhile (as in benchmarking), criterion-based methods can also be very useful for decision making. In fact, my experience suggests that it is often easier to gain buy-in at the departmental and college levels when criterion-based targets are established in concert with those being evaluated by such standards: faculty and deans. For instance, a unit or institution may be able to unilaterally define an a priori goal regarding certain ratios—for example, undergraduate SCH per FTE tenured or tenure-track faculty—without the need for external benchmarking or comparisons. A more common example is establishing a criterion for faculty salaries (such as 70 percent of the Oklahoma State University salary study average for that discipline and rank). The Oklahoma State University Salary study is a national study of faculty salaries conducted annually. The majority of institutions that participate in the study are public. The data are presented by discipline and rank, and are now also broken down by CIP code and Carnegie Classification. It is in its 33rd year of publication. Different institutional decision-making needs and situations may call for a mix-and-match approach to establishing performance criteria.

Before concluding, it is essential to return to the idea of institutional data and consider the notion of openly sharing cost and faculty data and information with varied stakeholders. Academic curiosity notwithstanding, the primary reasons behind examining integrated higher education cost data and human resource faculty data often have to do with investigations into a unit's or individual's productivity, efficiency, and cost-effectiveness. Such studies have the potential to lead to broad discussions and sound decisions regarding allocation and reallocation of resources, be they financial or human in nature. As such, I believe that it is essential to make data and information available to those stakeholders affected and to make them easily accessible as well. The two often do not go hand in hand, such as in the case of the availability of faculty salaries.

If organizational units and individuals understand how they are being evaluated and by what general metrics such evaluations are being based, they may take notice and reexamine their behaviors or their organizational values. Moreover, with time, one might find that organizational cultures shift, albeit gradually and slowly, and that certain aspects of the performance measurement might be embraced or at least accepted. At the very least, it is only reasonable to let people, and units of people, understand how and why certain decisions affecting their work lives and careers occur. Unlike in the past, lack of access to integrated higher education cost and human resource faculty data can no longer be blamed solely on limitations of information technology.

References

Armstrong, K. "Building a Consistent and Reliable Expenditure Database." In M. Middaugh (ed.), *Analyzing Costs in Higher Education: What Institutional Researchers Need to Know*. New Directions for Institutional Research, no. 106. San Francisco: Jossey-Bass, 2000.
Arreola, R. *Developing a Comprehensive Faculty Evaluation System*. Bolton, Mass.: Anker, 2000.
Barr, M. *Academic Administrator's Guide to Budgets and Financial Management*. San Francisco: Jossey-Bass, 2002.

Birnbaum, R. *Management Fads in Higher Education: Where They Come From, What They Do, Why They Fail.* San Francisco: Jossey-Bass, 2005.

Bowen, H. *The Costs of Higher Education.* San Francisco: Jossey-Bass, 1980.

Brinkman, P. "Factors Affecting Instructional Costs at Major Research Universities." *Journal of Higher Education,* 1981, 52(3), 265–279.

Brinkman, P. "The Economics of Higher Education: Focus on Cost." In M. Middaugh (ed.), *Analyzing Costs in Higher Education: What Institutional Researchers Need to Know.* New Directions for Institutional Research, no. 106. San Francisco: Jossey-Bass, 2000.

Brinkman, P., and Allen, R. "Concepts of Cost and Cost Analysis in Higher Education." *AIR Professional File,* 1986, 23, 1–8.

Brown, W., and Gaber, C. "Cost Containment in Higher Education: Issues and Recommendations." *ERIC Higher Education Report,* 2002, 28, 5.

Dyke, F. "Understanding Expenditure Data." In M. Middaugh (ed.), *Analyzing Costs in Higher Education: What Institutional Researchers Need to Know.* New Directions for Institutional Research, no. 106. San Francisco: Jossey-Bass, 2000.

Gater D., and Lombardi, J. "The Use of IPEDS /AAUP Faculty Data in Institutional Peer Comparisons." Sept. 2001. Retrieved Mar. 15, 2008, from http://thecenter.ufl.edu.

Hample, S. "Cost Studies in Higher Education." *AIR Professional File,* 1980, 7, 1–4.

Kaplan, R., and Norton, D. *The Balanced Scorecard.* Boston: Harvard Business School Press, 1996.

Kaplan, R., and Norton, D. *The Strategy-Focused Organization: How Balanced Scorecard Companies Thrive in the New Business Environment.* Boston: Harvard Business School Press, 2001.

Matier, M., Sidle, C., and Hurst, P. "Institutional Researchers' Roles in the Twenty-First Century." In T. Sanford, (ed.), *Preparing for the Information Needs of the Twenty-First Century.* New Directions for Institutional Research, no. 85. San Francisco: Jossey-Bass, 1995.

Middaugh, M. "Using Comparative Cost Data." In M. Middaugh (ed.), *Analyzing Costs in Higher Education: What Institutional Researchers Need to Know.* New Directions for Institutional Research, no. 106. San Francisco: Jossey-Bass, 2000.

Middaugh, M. *Understanding Faculty Productivity: Standards and Benchmarks for Colleges and Universities.* San Francisco: Jossey-Bass, 2001.

Middaugh, M. "Understanding Higher Education Costs." *Planning for Higher Education,* 2005, 33(3), 5–18.

Middaugh, M., Graham, R., and Shahid, A. *A Study of Higher Education Instructional Expenditures: The Delaware Study of Instructional Costs and Productivity.* Washington, D.C.: Institute of Education Sciences, 2003.

Middaugh, M., and Isaacs, H. "Benchmarking Departmental Activity via a Consortial Approach: The Delaware Study." In J. Groccia and J. Miller (eds.), *On Becoming a Productive University: Strategies for Reducing Costs and Increasing Quality in Higher Education.* Bolton, Mass.: Anker, 2005.

Milam, J. "Cost of Instruction: Research and Praxis." 2008. Retrieved Mar. 5, 2008, from http://highered.org/.

Minter, J. "Using Ratio Analysis to Evaluate Financial Performance." In C. Frances (ed.), *Successful Responses to Financial Difficulties.* New Directions for Higher Education, no. 38. San Francisco: Jossey-Bass, 1982.

Nelson, M. "Breaking Out of the IT Silo: The Integration Maturity Model." EDUCAUSE Center for Applied Research, Research Bulletin, 2005, 6, 1–10.

Oklahoma State University Salary study. Retrieved Mar. 1, 2008, from http://vpaf.okstate.edu/irim/FacultySalary.html

Sanders, L. "The Future IR Office." In Sanders, L. (ed.), *How Technology Is Changing Institutional Research.* New Directions for Institutional Research, no. 103. San Francisco: Jossey-Bass, 1999.

Simpson, W. *Cost Containment for Higher Education: Strategies for Public Policy and Institutional Administration.* Westport, Conn.: Praeger, 1991.

Volkwein, J. "The Four Faces of Institutional Research." In Volkwein, J. (ed.), *What is Institutional Research All About? A Critical and Comprehensive Assessment of the Profession.* New Directions for Institutional Research, no. 104. San Francisco: Jossey-Bass, 1999.

Winston, G. C. "A Guide to Measuring College Costs." In M. Middaugh (ed.), *Analyzing Costs in Higher Education: What Institutional Researchers Need to Know.* New Directions for Institutional Research, no. 106. San Francisco: Jossey-Bass, 2000.

GARY D. LEVY is associate vice provost for institutional research and assessment and a professor of psychology at Marquette University.

A four-step statistical process is proposed to take faculty compensation analysis from identification of possible inequities to potential salary adjustment options.

A Four-Step Faculty Compensation Model: From Equity Analysis to Adjustment

Serge Herzog

Among the varied analytical challenges institutional researchers face, examining faculty pay may be one of the most vexing. Although the literature on faculty compensation analysis dates back to the 1970s (Loeb and Ferber, 1971; Gordon, Morton, and Braden, 1974; Scott, 1977; Braskamp and Johnson, 1978; McLaughlin, Smart, and Montgomery, 1978), both conceptual and operational questions on how to identify, and correct for, inequity in pay persist. Similarly, there is no dominant approach to ensure faculty compensation reflects changing market conditions. Thus, the dual goal of fashioning compensation analysis to screen for both internal equity and external calibration in pay faces a number of challenges. After briefly addressing these, this chapter lays out four steps that could be used in a compensation model for instructional faculty at a public land grant university.

Methodological Issues

In addition to ensuring that quality faculty are attracted and retained, institutions conduct compensation analyses in order to identify possible pay inequities associated with faculty gender, race, ethnicity, age, national origin, or religion. Fair treatment along these attributes is federally mandated and codified in the Equal Pay Act of 1963 and Title VII of the Civil Rights Act of 1964 and its 1972 amendment. Unequal pay may not constitute a

NEW DIRECTIONS FOR INSTITUTIONAL RESEARCH, no. 140, Winter 2008 © Wiley Periodicals, Inc.
Published online in Wiley InterScience (www.interscience.wiley.com) • DOI: 10.1002/ir.269

legal violation, however, if the cause is due to seniority, merit, job productivity, or a systematically applied factor other than the above-listed personal attributes (Moore, 1993).

To examine these issues, analysts typically employ multiple regression models, incorporating factors (variables) identified in human capital theory that determine individual productivity (Oaxaca, 1973; Neumark, 1988; Toutkoushian, 2002). Unfortunately, salary regression models are often affected by problems such as omitted variable bias due to lack of data, selection bias associated with measures of career progression, or statistical estimation bias due to sequential testing of the same predictor variable in multiequation models.

An example of omitted variable bias is the exclusion of a measure of faculty productivity or performance that may be captured on the basis of publication record, grant-supported research, or quality of teaching. For example, the following institutions did not incorporate a productivity measure based on a review of their equity studies posted online: University of California–Irvine, University of California–Davis, New York University, University of Illinois at Urbana–Champaign, Emory University, and North Carolina State University (Herzog, 2005). Such data may not be available, however, and if so, constructing a transparent, properly weighted index or scale that reflects the relative importance of different contributions across academic units poses a formidable challenge to institutional researchers (Weistroffer, Spinelli, Canavos, and Fuhs, 2001). Hence, measures are usually limited to publication or citation record (Strathman, 2000; Graves, Marchand, and Sexton, 2002; Loeb, 2003; Barbezat, 2004) and do not reflect contributions in teaching, research grants, community outreach, or other dimensions that may be valued by the institution. To obviate the limitation of a narrow performance measure, some studies incorporate rating scales used in annual faculty evaluation administered by supervisors or faculty peers (Carlin and Rooney, 2000), or they include an average performance indicator derived from merit-based salary increases (Duncan, Krall, Maxey, and Prus, 2004).

Another source of omitted variable bias is the lack of consideration of external market- or discipline-based influences on compensation at the institutional level. Typically the effect of market forces is accounted for by inclusion of a market ratio (comparable market salary to institutional salary), dummy variables for separate academic disciplines, or geographical location for multi-institution studies (Balzer and others, 1996; Haignere, 2002; Barbezat and Hughes, 2005). A recent study suggested that a single continuous metric, such as a ratio indicator, may yield a better-fitting parsimonious model without sacrificing explanatory power (Luna, 2007). Preferably, however, one should control for both external and internal influences on compensation within a discipline by including a market factor as well as department or academic program affiliation. Ehrenberg, McGraw, and Mrdjenovic (2006) show that variance in the quality of faculty across institutions is associated with significant salary differentials within a discipline.

Selection bias associated with measures of career progression may occur when variables for rank or tenure status are used to estimate faculty salary. Both rank and tenure status may be biased if the process of promotion to tenure or higher rank is not administered fairly across all members of the faculty (Haignere, 2002). Attention in the literature has been focused mostly on how the inclusion of rank or tenure status may underestimate gender-based bias in pay.

Boudreau and others (1997) tested this proposition with data free of gender bias, using predicted salaries of female faculty derived from coefficients of a male-only regression model. Deletion of rank and years in rank from that model yielded a false-negative effect associated with female gender, which disappeared after including the rank information. Strathman (2000) tested the rank effect endogenously, using an instrumental variable (IV) estimator of rank in a second-stage regression model. He observed little confoundedness in rank and gender, but cautioned that IV models may not yield accurate estimates due to paucity of factors that predict rank but are unrelated to salary. Becker and Toutkoushian (2003) employed a similar approach to correct for selection bias into full professor rank. Having inserted a Heckit estimator to adjust for the probability of full professor rank, they found a persistent influence of gender on salary, though with a small change in effect size compared to the unadjusted rank-based model. To account for multiple forms of possible pay discrimination, Toutkoushian, Bellas, and Moore (2007) estimated the interaction effects of faculty gender, race, and marital status. Data from the 1999 National Study of Postsecondary Faculty covering over eight hundred institutions revealed limited evidence of significant interactions among these three attributes. This finding may yield little guidance for institutional studies due to the sparseness of data when faculty members are disaggregated across all three attributes. Interpreting higher-order interaction effects poses an added challenge in single-equation models.

To obviate limitations of the single-equation model, some studies stratify faculty by gender and other attributes and estimate the influence of each sequentially (Ashraf, 1996; Bellas, 1993). Estimating the influence of gender, race, and marital status—or any other potential source of discrimination such as age, religion, or national origin—would require a series or regressions. This may substantially increase the type 1, or "experimentwise," error—leading to a significant finding where there is none—when the same variables are used repeatedly in independent tests. Moreover, the simultaneous effect of multiple factors that describe professional and personal attributes of academic faculty may not be captured adequately where only one outcome is examined at a time. For example, promotion to higher rank may be correlated with a combination of both personal and professional attributes. These attributes may interact in ways that are identified more easily with a multivariate design that can accommodate the presence of multiple causes and effects typified by the complexity of human behavior (Fish, 1988).

Analytical Approach

Mindful of limitations associated with omitted variable bias, selection bias resulting from measures of career progression, and estimation bias due to multiple testing of the same predictor variables, this study lays out a four-step process to identify and control for possible biases in compensation and proposes a framework for salary adjustment aimed at ensuring performance-based internal and external equity. Following guidance in previous research that recommends identification of possible systematic inequity due to personal attributes and rank or tenure promotion prior to specification of the final regression model (Boudreau and others, 1997; Moore, 1993; Fogel, 1986), the first three steps determine whether personal attributes that may be a source of pay inequity should be incorporated in the final compensation adjustment model. Accordingly, the following statistical analyses are performed:

1. Canonical correlation to identify possible bias associated with age, gender, and ethnicity/race
2. Binary logistic regression to identify possible bias in tenure promotion
3. Multinomial logistic regression to identify possible bias in rank promotion
4. Multiple linear regression to identify possible inequity in compensation

The first step is designed to identify the degree of correlation between personal and professional attributes of the academic faculty that may suggest the presence of systematic discrimination. To this end, canonical correlation creates synthetic (or latent) variables out of all personal attribute variables (age, gender, ethnicity/race) and one out of all professional attribute variables (rank, tenure status, years at institution, academic field, and so on) on the basis of a linear equation for each variable set in order to maximize the correlation between the synthetic variables, which is the canonical correlation. (For a technical treatment of canonical correlation, see Tabachnick and Fidell, 2007, and Stevens, 2002.) The canonical solution is then examined for any significant correlation between individual personal attributes and professional attributes within each significant canonical function (or root) to determine the presence of discriminatory bias.

The second step looks at faculty members with tenure or tenure-track status and determines if those not yet tenured should be considered for tenure promotion on the basis of misclassification in the logistic regression model. Specifically, does the information used in the model to predict tenure status suggest a case of delayed or denied tenure? Similarly, the third step examines misclassified cases where the predicted rank is higher than a faculty member's actual rank. Since rank includes more than two possible outcomes, a multinomial solution is required. Cases identified in steps 2 and 3 that deserve further consideration may be removed from the data file before proceeding with step 4. Results from both the canonical correlation analysis and regression govern whether faculty age, gender, or ethnicity/race are included in the final model of step 4. That model should be as parsimonious as possible and preferably should exclude variables measuring personal attributes that are not legitimate determinants of faculty compensation.

Academic Faculty Data

I now describe how this four-step process works using data from a single institution. Information on members of the instructional faculty originated with the institution's human resource office that keeps a census-based snapshot file of all employees for each fall and spring term. The working file for this study includes all regular-contract faculty members with a full-time appointment during fall 2005 and at least two years of instructional employment at the institution, yielding data for 675 cases. All members of the faculty included in the analysis were contacted to validate and verify the accuracy of the data. Table 4.1 furnishes a description of the variables used in the analyses.

Table 4.1 Variables Used in the Salary Analyses

Variable	Description
Age	Age in years as of spring 2006
Gender[a]	Male or female
Ethnicity/race[a]	White, Asian, Native American, black, Hispanic, foreign
Highest Degree[a]	Doctorate, master's, bachelor's
Terminal Degree[a]	Yes, No
YrswTermDegr	Number of years with terminal degree
Appointment type[a]	Tenured, tenure track, non-tenure track
Years with tenure	Number of years with tenure
Hired rank[a]	Professor, associate, assistant, instructor
Current rank[a]	Professor, associate, assistant, instructor
Years in rank[b]	Number of years at a rank (professor, associate, assistant, instructor)
Longevity	Number of years at institution
Current salary	Logarithm of 2005–06 annual salary (12 months/9 months = 0.818)
Merit rating	Average merit rating for past five years
Market Factor	Market factor (OSU salary/current salary)
MarketFacBus	Market factor (OSU + AACSB salary/current salary)
Discipline[a]	Humanities, engineering, math/science, business, natural science, preprofessional, fine arts, social science, health science, education

[a]Dummy variable (0, 1).

[b]Continuous metric for each rank.

NEW DIRECTIONS FOR INSTITUTIONAL RESEARCH • DOI: 10.1002/ir

Actual salaries were converted into natural logarithm-based values to correct for curve linearity associated with accelerated rise in senior-level compensation. This conversion is particularly appropriate at institutions where salaries are affected by routine percentage-based increases, such as cost-of-living adjustments, or when the range of compensation from high to low is substantial. Although a semilog model yields coefficients no longer expressed in dollar values, predicted log-based salaries can be converted back to a dollar scale when considering pay adjustments. Salaries of faculty on twelve-month contracts were recalculated to be consistent with those on nine-month contracts.

The market factor represents the ratio of the average salary at comparable institutions for the corresponding academic field and rank to the actual salary. The Oklahoma State University (OSU) salary survey furnished data for all other forty-nine land grant universities used in calculating the market factor. To reflect the difference in purchasing power between institutional salaries and the OSU survey-based market average, the former were adjusted based on the average cost of living index difference to the other forty-nine localities. In response to a request from faculty affiliated with the college of business, market factors for their faculty are based on data from the Association to Advance Collegiate Schools of Business (AACSB), although the final model in step 4 could have used both sources for separate estimates.

Faculty performance at the institution was measured on the basis of the average merit rating for the past five years, or a minimum of two to four years for those with less than five years of employment. As stipulated in the institutional by-laws, the rating reflects faculty accomplishments in teaching, scholarly and creative activity, professional organizations, and service to the institution. Some departments used peer-based evaluation coupled with one rendered from a supervisor to approximate a 360-degree review before arriving at an annual rating. The monetary value of 1 merit point on the merit scale did not fluctuate significantly during the period captured due to a stable size in annual merit pool dollars, thus preserving the merit scale as a reasonably useful predictor of salary received.

Measuring Systematic Bias

Identification of possible systematic bias in faculty pay focused on three factors: age, gender, and ethnicity/race. Marital status, religion, national origin, and other personal attributes could not be analyzed in a similar fashion due to lack of available data. The multivariate shared relationship between the two variable sets (personal versus professional attributes) yielded seven functions with squared canonical correlations (R_c^2) of .693, .243, .092, .060, .045, .034, and .009. Collectively, the explained variance between personal and professional attributes across all functions was statistically significant (F [182, 4271] = 6.72; $p < .001$) and amounted to approximately 82 percent of the total variation (Wilks' λ = .18). Results from the dimension reduction analysis in Table 4.2 reveal that the first three functions are statistically significant, though the third one yields only 9.2 percent of explained variance (as indicated above) due to the orthogonal nature of functions. Hence, only the first two functions are retained to discern the individual contribution of personal and professional attributes to the multivariate correlation. They explain 69 percent and 24 percent of the variance within their respective canonical function.

Applying a common threshold for statistical significance in factor analyses, structure coefficients (r_s) with a minimum absolute value of .40 are in bold in Table 4.3 (Sherry and Henson, 2005). The squared structure coefficients measure the proportion of shared variance between the observed variable and the synthetic construct, while the communality coefficients (h^2) indicate the sum of shared variance of all functions in the canonical solution.

The first function shows that age is positively correlated with senior rank (full professor), years in senior rank, being tenured, years with tenure, and years with terminal degree. Conversely, age is negatively correlated with junior rank (assistant professor) and pretenure status, with both structure coefficient values pointing in the opposite direction (having a positive value). These correlations are expected, as they reflect typical time-related progression in professional status. The second canonical function reveals that females are less likely than males to be in engineering and math- or science-related fields, and they are less likely to hold a doctorate as their highest degree, and, instead, are more likely to hold a master's degree. The first result is expected, as the pool of females entering the physical sciences, though growing, is still too small to make up for long-standing male representation. Inverse correlation on holding the doctorate may be related to fields popular with women that do not offer a doctorate degree. Alternatively, women with master's degrees may enter higher education at a greater rate than similarly degreed men (if so, it may warrant further examination to ensure no bias exists in hiring decisions). No other significant correlations involving age, gender, or ethnicity/race emerged from the canonical

Table 4.2. Dimension Reduction Data for Canonical Functions

Roots	Wilks' λ	F	Hypothetical df	Error df	Significance of F
1 to 7	0.18	6.72	182	4,271	0.000
2 to 7	0.59	2.32	150	3,691	0.000
3 to 7	0.78	1.34	120	3,101	0.009
4 to 7	0.86	1.06	92	2,500	0.326
5 to 7	0.91	0.88	66	1,888	0.748
6 to 7	0.96	0.67	42	1,266	0.949
7 to 7	0.99	0.29	20	634	0.999

Table 4.3. Canonical Solution for Age, Gender, Ethnicity/Race Predicting Professional Attributes

Variable	Funtion 1			Function 2			
	Coefficient	r_s	r_s^2 (%)	Coefficient	r_s	r_s^2 (%)	h^2 (%)
Assistant	−0.062	**0.558**	31.136	−0.014	−0.019	0.036	31.17
Associate	−0.143	0.002	0.000	−0.131	−0.137	1.877	1.88
Professor	−0.153	**−0.637**	40.577	−0.121	0.225	5.063	**45.64**
Years as professor	−0.076	**−0.699**	48.860	0.008	0.205	4.203	**53.06**
Years as assistant	−0.189	−0.157	2.465	−0.208	−0.154	2.372	4.84
Years as associate	−0.054	**−0.462**	21.344	−0.089	−0.016	0.026	21.37
Hired assistant	0.087	0.311	9.672	0.156	0.144	2.074	11.75
Hired associate	−0.130	−0.289	8.352	−0.025	−0.047	0.221	8.57
Hired professor	−0.179	−0.373	13.913	0.112	0.176	3.098	17.01
Ten-track	0.107	**0.508**	25.806	0.212	0.077	0.593	26.40
Tenured	0.177	**−0.558**	31.136	0.464	0.200	4.000	35.14
Years tenured	−0.323	**−0.770**	59.290	0.177	0.172	2.958	**62.25**
Master's	0.638	0.119	1.416	−0.249	**−0.428**	18.318	19.73
Doctorate	0.682	−0.097	0.941	−0.130	**0.431**	18.576	19.52
Years with term degree	−0.541	**−0.877**	76.913	−0.095	0.111	1.232	**78.15**
Average merit	0.108	−0.124	1.538	−0.110	0.085	0.723	2.26
Market factor	0.022	0.163	2.657	0.217	0.071	0.504	3.16
Engineering	−0.097	−0.003	0.001	0.446	**0.451**	20.340	20.34
Math/science	−0.075	0.011	0.012	0.529	**0.465**	21.623	21.63
Business	−0.105	−0.001	0.000	0.197	0.164	2.690	2.69
Nat science	−0.112	−0.055	0.303	0.164	0.009	0.008	0.31
Preprofessor	−0.064	−0.030	0.090	−0.238	−0.301	9.060	9.15
Fine arts	−0.041	0.027	0.073	0.066	−0.008	0.006	0.08
Social science	−0.105	−0.033	0.109	−0.143	−0.259	6.708	6.82
Health science	−0.164	−0.015	0.023	−0.268	−0.371	13.764	13.79
Education	−0.154	−0.038	0.144	−0.211	−0.271	7.344	7.49
R_c^2			69.30			24.30	
Age	−0.960	**−0.983**	96.629	−0.261	−0.162	2.624	**99.25**
Female	0.158	0.288	8.294	−0.947	**−0.913**	83.357	**91.65**
Asian	−0.035	0.025	0.063	0.254	0.304	9.242	9.30
Hispanic	0.078	0.151	2.280	−0.006	−0.022	0.048	2.33
Black	−0.006	0.024	0.058	−0.012	−0.051	0.260	0.32
Native American	0.012	0.076	0.578	0.150	0.102	1.040	1.62
Foreign	−0.009	0.092	0.846	−0.004	0.048	0.230	1.08

Note: Structure coefficients (r_s) greater than $|.40|$ are in bold. Communality coefficients (h_2) greater than 40 percent are in bold. Coefficients = standardized canonical function coefficient. r_s = structure coefficient. Cases processed: 675 (excluding medical school faculty).

functions. The structure coefficient for being female is significant (–.913) in the second function, but no promotion-related professional attributes (such as rank, tenure status, or years in either) comprising that function rise to the level of conventional significance (±|.40|). Thus, there is no statistical evidence for systematic undue influence of these measured personal attributes on the professional characteristics included in the subsequent estimation models.

Results from the canonical correlation analysis guide the model specification in the second step: estimation of tenure status. Accordingly, age, gender, and ethnicity/race are dropped due to their insignificance in the first step and following the rule that personal attributes must not determine tenure promotion. A binomial logistic regression model estimates tenure status on the basis of the remaining variables. Of the 590 faculty members with tenure or tenure-track status, the model misclassified nine, five on tenure track who were predicted to be tenured. Overall, the correct classification rate was 98.5 percent with good model fit (Nagelkerke R^2 = .95; HosmerLemeshow decile accuracy significance = .99). The parameter estimate information is available from the author.

Table 4.4 depicts five hypothetical cases to illustrate what could be gleaned from the characteristics of each case to explain the misclassification. First, none of them were initially hired as tenure-track assistant

Table 4.4 Hypothetical Characteristics of Misclassified Tenure-Status Cases

Employee ID	Department	Current Rank	Age	Gender	Ethnicity/ Race	Hire Degree	Average Merit
101	U	Assistant professor	43	M	White	Ph.D.	1
102	W	Assistant professor	42	F	Asian	Ph.D.	3.75
103	Z	Associate professor	44	M	White	Ph.D.	2.75
104	X	Professor	46	F	White	Ph.D.	4.25
105	Y	Professor	57	M	White	Ph.D.	1.25

Employee ID	Current Degree	Term Degree	Year of Degree	Hire Rank	Years at Institution	Years Assistant	Years Associate	Years Professor
101	Ph.D.	Yes	1992	Nonregular	11	11	0	0
102	Ph.D.	Yes	1995	Instructor	9	8	0	0
103	Ph.D.	Yes	1964	Associate professor	3	0	3	0
104	Ph.D.	Yes	1986	Professor	4	0	0	4
105	Ph.D.	Yes	1978	Professor	2	0	0	2

professors, the typical starting point to embark for tenure promotion at an institution. The first employee (ID 101) has a low average merit rating and started on a nonregular contract, thus spending part of the recorded years at the assistant professor on a nontenure track. This may explain why the person is not yet tenured. The second case (ID 102) deserves closer consideration, given the high merit rating and many years at the assistant professor level. The other three employees were hired at a rank that typically confers tenure. They too should receive additional scrutiny. The ensuing process of determining whether those identified using the prediction model should be tenured must be informed by other relevant information that may have not been incorporated in the formal analysis. Thus, the model serves as a starting point in that endeavor.

Similar to tenure status prediction, a multinomial logistic regression model estimated the rank of all members of the instructional faculty, again using the variables in Table 4.1 minus age, gender, and ethnicity/race characteristics. That model yielded a 98.6 percent correct classification rate, with twelve misclassified rank cases. Of those, only three involved members with a lower rank than predicted. One faculty member had a low five-year average merit rating, and another lacked the terminal degree for that discipline. All three cases were referred for further consideration.

Determining Salary Adjustment

To identify possible salary inequities beyond those associated with age, gender, and ethnicity/race, the analysis proceeded with a multiple linear regression models for all nonmedical school faculty. This final step has the dual purpose of furnishing insights on the correlates of faculty compensation and providing a starting point for determination of salary adjustment. Hence, a judicious balance between explanatory and predictive power governs specification of the regression model. While the latter can be assessed with the standard error of estimate (SEE)—the average distance of the predicted from the actual salary—the former typically requires some appraisal of the orthogonality of the predictor variables or verification of the level of their collinearity. After identifying statistical outliers based on standardized residuals and Cook's distance, the model excluded predictors associated with unacceptably high communality in the variance decomposition matrix, following established criteria (Cohen, Cohen, West, and Aiken, 2003; Pedhazur, 1997). Insertion of quadratic terms for time-related variables (including years in rank or at institution) failed to improve model fit.

Parameter estimates for the salary prediction of nonmedical school faculty are listed in Table 4.5. The model explains over 90 percent of the variation in salary (R^2 = .94), on average predicts the actual annual salary within $4,740 (SEE), and suggests that seniority (professor rank), market influence (market factor), and certain fields (business, engineering) weigh most heavily on level of compensation. Merit rating is the next most important factor,

NEW DIRECTIONS FOR INSTITUTIONAL RESEARCH • DOI: 10.1002/ir

Table 4.5 Parameter Estimates to Predict Faculty Salary

	Parameter Estimate	Standard Error	Beta Coefficient	t-Ratio	Significance	VIF
Intercept	17.870	0.272		65.81	***	
Master's degree	−0.033	0.011	−0.041	−2.98	**	1.95
Bachelor's degree	−0.038	0.043	−0.010	−0.88		1.30
Years with terminal degree	0.001	0.000	0.029	1.81		2.80
Non-tenure track	−0.010	0.011	−0.013	−0.88		2.15
Hired as instructor	0.002	0.013	0.003	0.17		2.22
Hired as associate professor	0.021	0.013	0.022	1.68		1.76
Hired as professor	0.048	0.017	0.039	2.78	**	2.09
Instructor	−0.284	0.018	−0.228	−15.56	***	2.25
Associate professor	0.170	0.013	0.240	13.06	***	3.57
Professor	0.407	0.018	0.576	22.99	***	6.60
Years as assistant professor	0.001	0.001	0.007	0.51		1.99
Years as associate professor	0.001	0.001	0.018	1.24		2.19
Years as professor	0.004	0.001	0.087	4.81	***	3.45
Average merit rating	0.044	0.005	0.114	8.67	***	1.82
Engineering	0.241	0.014	0.219	17.41	***	1.66
Math/physical sciences	0.102	0.012	0.123	8.76	***	2.09
Business	0.395	0.015	0.305	25.57	***	1.50
Natural sciences	0.053	0.013	0.055	4.19	***	1.83
Preprofessional fields	0.151	0.020	0.101	7.60	***	1.85
Fine arts	0.000	0.018	0.000	−0.01		1.29
Social sciences	0.077	0.013	0.076	5.94	***	1.72
Health sciences	0.146	0.021	0.074	6.80	***	1.26
Education	0.053	0.015	0.043	3.62	***	1.52
Market factor	−7.046	0.268	−0.338	−26.32	***	1.74

Note: Dependent variable is the logarithm of annual salary (excluding medical school). Reference categories: Doctoral degree, hired as assistant professor, assistant professor, humanities. Model summary: Adjusted R^2 = .94; F-ratio = 411.76***; N = 675.
*** $p \le .001$; ** $p \le .01$.

indicating that individual job performance matters significantly in the determination of salary. Removal of variables measuring years in tenure, being tenured, and years of employment at the institution yielded more acceptable levels of collinearity. To further warrant the exclusion of personal attributes from the final salary prediction model, marginal effects of age, gender, and ethnicity/race are listed in Table 4.6. None of these attributes contributes significantly to the model, rendering the parsimonious solution preferable.

Although results from multiple regression models should not be used for mechanistic salary adjustments (Haignere, 2002)—results merely yield

Table 4.6. Contribution of Faculty Personal Attributes to Salary Prediction Model

Model	Adjusted R^2	Standard Error of Estimate	R^2 Change	F Change	df	Significant F Change
			Marginal Effect			
Full model	0.938	0.084				
Minus age	0.936	0.084	0.000	3.68	1	0.06
Minus gender	0.937	0.083	0.000	1.10	1	0.29
Minus ethnicity/race	0.937	0.083	–0.001	1.32	5	0.26
Minus age, gender, ethnicity/race	0.937	0.083	–0.001	1.22	7	0.29

systematic differences in pay associated with group membership—the approach used here provides a starting point to identify those most likely in need of adjustment and offers several options to determine the adjustment amount. Stewart, Dalton, Dino, and Wilkinson (1996) chronicle how one institution rationalized an across-the-board adjustment for individuals below the lower limit of a specified salary goal using a value-centered prescriptive model. Gaylord and McLaughlin (1991) propose adjustments on the basis of the average negative residual for members of specific groups (such as by college, department, or rank), whereby individuals' salaries would be augmented by the residual amount (difference between average actual salary and average predicted salary for that group). This class-based approach, affecting all members within a group, could be coupled with discretionary input from deans or department heads who may look at an individual's job performance as reflected in annual evaluations (Snyder, Hyer, and McLaughlin, 1994). Alternatively, instead of relying on statistical regression, Sun (2002) recommends an additive model encompassing all relevant criteria judged by the institution to influence compensation in order to arrive at a projected salary. In turn, those underpaid in relation to the projected salary may receive an adjustment governed by matching the total amount needed for corrections with the available amount of resources.

The development of salary adjustment criteria in this study is informed by the cited research, but emphasis is placed on offering alternative ways to determine the amount of compensation adjustment and identify individuals deserving them. First, recognizing the significant effect of market factor on predicted salary, the salary prediction model may use several sources for market salary information. In addition to the OSU survey, the College and University Professional Association, the Association of American Medical Colleges, and the Association to Advance Collegiate Schools of Business furnish market salary data for their respective domains. Use of multiple sources ensures that external equity measures reflect compensation levels within certain academic fields as closely as possible. This study constructed the market factor from OSU survey data, but also inserted market data from other sources in separate estimation models to triangulate predicted salary.

"Underpaid" individuals were identified initially as those with actual salaries below 90 percent of the predicted amount, yielding a pool of forty-seven to fifty-three individuals depending on the source of the market data. After removing several statistical outliers (±2 standard error), the remaining candidates required a total dollar amount to raise their salaries to the 90 percent mark that was beyond the level set aside for equity correction. To bring the two into balance, the institutional research office, in consultation with the salary equity committee, the human resource office, and the budget office, proposed the following criteria for salary adjustment eligibility and amount: (1) current salary had to be lower than the market salary for that individual, (2) the average merit rating had to be higher than the average for the person's department or academic unit, and (3) the adjustment amount could be no larger than 10 percent of the current salary. Application of all three screens rendered the total required adjustment amount eminently fundable, having shrunk the eligible pool down to eight cases. This also opened up room for discretionary input from deans and department heads to raise salaries to the 90 percent mark in cases where the 10-percent-of-salary limit was not enough.

If consistently administered to all faculty members, selection screens offer the institutional researcher the opportunity to generate alternative outcomes to fit different funding scenarios. In developing selection screens, the institutional researcher seeks consensus from key stakeholders (department heads, deans, senior administrators) to establish a fair, transparent, and rational process in determining who should receive salary adjustments and how large the adjustments should be. The multistep process laid out here that may culminate in the salary adjustment for some is designed to promote internal and external equity and to nurture a sense of fairness in compensation among colleagues while heightening their awareness of the institution's commitment to stay competitive with trends in the market.

Caveats and Summary

Thorough analysis of faculty compensation requires that the researcher have a good grasp of the factors that influence the institutional award structure and relate to recognition of individual achievement within an academic field. The comprehensive capture of these factors should be reflected in the specification of the salary model (Moore, 1993; Toutkoushian, 2002). Although no model completely eliminates bias due to omitted variables, inclusion of relevant information on professional status (rank, tenure, field), experience (years in rank/tenured), performance (evaluation of teaching/ research record), and relative level of compensation compared to outside peers (market factor) yields regression models that typically explain 70 to

90 percent of the variance in instructional faculty salaries when using data from a single institution.

This study recommends that possible inequities associated with personal attributes be identified prior to estimation of a salary correction amount. Focus should be centered not only on gender but other personal attributes covered under the law, as well as other sources of bias that may lead to inequity in pay (including marital status). To statistically cope with the simultaneity of multiple causes and effects between several sources of potential discriminatory bias and a host of professional attributes and experiences, a multivariate method of analysis is deemed more appropriate than a univariate technique measuring one outcome variable at a time. The application of canonical correlation analysis in this study illustrates such an approach in order to gauge that complexity in variable interaction. A multivariate approach also minimizes the risk of committing a type 1 error, the likelihood of generating a significant finding when there is none, which is more likely to occur in serial regression models.

If the multivariate model produces no evidence of systematic bias associated with personal attributes, these variables can be removed from subsequent analyses. Thus, the researcher can proceed with a more parsimonious model to identify potential cases of delayed rank or tenure promotion. Such cases may be deleted, or corrected on the basis of further evaluation, before submitting the data file for analysis of who might be underpaid. This final step in the compensation analysis is designed to provide a starting point in determining cases of salary adjustment and the size of the adjustment. To this end, the predicted salary generated from the regression model may serve as an indication of whether someone is underpaid in relation to prevailing compensation in a comparable position elsewhere or to others at the same institution. In the latter case, one may use job performance, as reflected in annual evaluation rating, to establish eligibility for pay adjustment. Proper position matching with outside salary surveys is critical in the former situation, where an accurate salary comparison may furnish the requisite evidence to justify an augmentation in pay. Whatever rational screening criteria are used, they must be applied consistently to all members of the faculty, and they should render the level and number of total salary adjustments fundable within the limits of available resources in both the short and long terms.

As proposed in this study, the inclusion of a job performance rating variable in both the salary prediction model and as a criterion for adjustment eligibility is strongly recommended. If an institution claims to compensate its faculty on the basis of productivity and contribution to the profession, one could scarcely afford to engage in a compensation analysis without taking into account job performance (Moore, 1993). While use of average merit rating may furnish a comprehensive indicator of job performance, such ratings may still reflect normative judgment and fail to impart the precision of counting publications, citations, or research awards. In trying to strike a balance between a broad, likely subjective measure on the one hand and a narrower, objective one on the other hand, the selection of a job performance indicator should be endorsed by the faculty in order for the compensation model to lead to acceptable salary adjustment decisions.

References

Ashraf, J. "The Influence of Gender on Faculty Salaries in the United States, 1969–89." *Applied Economics,* 1996, *28*(7), 857–864.

Balzer, W., and others. "Critical Modeling Principles When Testing for Gender Equity in Faculty Salary." *Research in Higher Education,* 1996, *37*(4), 633–658.

Barbezat, D. "A Loyalty Tax? National Measures of Academic Salary Compression." *Research in Higher Education,* 2004, *45*(7), 761–776.

Barbezat, D., and Hughes, J. "Salary Structure Effects and the Gender Pay Gap in Academia." *Research in Higher Education,* 2005, *46*(6), 621–640.

Becker, W., and Toutkoushian, R. "Measuring Gender Bias in the Salaries of Tenured Faculty Members." In R. Toutkoushian (ed.), *Unresolved Issues in Conducting Salary-Equity Studies.* New Directions for Institutional Research, no. 117. San Francisco: Jossey-Bass, 2003.

Bellas, M. "Faculty Salaries: Still a Cost of Being Female?" *Social Science Quarterly,* 1993, *74*(1), 62–75.

Boudreau, N., and others. "Should Faculty Rank Be Included as a Predictor Variable in Studies of Gender Equity in University Faculty Salaries?" *Research in Higher Education,* 1997, *38*(3), 297–312.

Braskamp, L., and Johnson, D. "The Use of a Parity-Equity Model to Evaluate Faculty Salary Policies." *Research in Higher Education,* 1978, *8*(1), 57–66.

Carlin, P., and Rooney, P. "Am I Paid Fairly?" *Change,* 2000, *32*(2), 40–50.

Cohen, J., Cohen, P., West, S., and Aiken, L. *Applied Multiple Regression/Correlation Analysis for the Behavioral Sciences.* (3rd ed.) Mahwah, N.J.: Erlbaum, 2003.

Duncan, K., Krall, L., Maxey, J., and Prus, M. "Faculty Productivity, Seniority, and Salary Compression." *Eastern Economic Journal,* 2004, *30*(2), 293–310.

Ehrenberg, R., McGraw, M., and Mrdjenovic, J. "Why Do Field Differentials in Average Faculty Salaries Vary Across Universities?" *Economics of Education Review,* 2006, *25,* 241–248.

Fish, L. "Why Multivariate Methods Are Usually Vital." *Measurement and Evaluation in Counseling and Development,* 1988, *21,* 130–137.

Fogel, W. "Class Pay Discrimination and Multiple Regression Proofs." *Nebraska Law Review,* 1986, *65,* 289–329.

Gaylord, C., and McLaughlin, G. "Adjusting Observations to Make Residuals of a Sub-Group Sum to Zero." VAS Chapter, American Statistical Association, Blacksburg, Va., May 1991.

Gordon, N., Morton, T., and Braden, I. "Faculty Salaries: Is There Discrimination by Sex, Race, and Discipline?" *American Economic Review,* 1974, *68*(3), 419–427.

Graves, P., Marchand, J., and Sexton, R. "Hedonic Wage Equations for Higher Education Faculty." *Economics of Education Review,* 2002, *21,* 491–496.

Haignere, L. *Paychecks: A Guide to Conducting Salary-Equity Studies for Higher Education Faculty.* Washington, D.C.: American Association of University Professors, 2002.

Herzog, S. "University Salaries as a Tool for Implementing Strategic Decisions." Paper presented at the European Association for Institutional Research Forum, Riga, Latvia, Aug. 2005.

Loeb, J. "Hierarchical Linear Modeling in Salary–Equity Studies." In R. Toutkoushian (ed.), *Unresolved Issues in Conducting Salary-Equity Studies.* New Directions for Institutional Research, no. 117. San Francisco: Jossey-Bass, 2003.

Loeb, J., and Ferber, M. "Sex as Predictive of Salary and Status on a University Faculty." *Journal of Educational Measurement,* 1971, *8*(4), 235–244.

Luna, A. "Using a Market Ratio Factor in Faculty Salary Equity Studies." *AIR Professional File,* Spring 2007, no. 103.

McLaughlin, G., Smart, J., and Montgomery, J. "Factors Which Comprise Salary." *Research in Higher Education,* 1978, *8,* 67–82.

Moore, N. "Faculty Salary Equity: Issues in Regression Model Selection." *Research in Higher Education,* 1993, *34*(1), 107–126.

Neumark, D. "Employers' Discriminatory Behaviour and the Estimation of Wage Discrimination." *Journal of Human Resources,* 1988, *23*(3), 279–295.

Oaxaca, R. "Male-Female Wage Differentials in Urban Labor Markets." *International Economic Review,* 1973, *14*(3), 693–709.

Pedhazur, E. *Multiple Regression in Behavioral Research.* Orlando, Fla.: Harcourt Brace, 1997.

Scott, E. *Higher Education Salary Evaluation Kit.* Washington, D.C.: American Association of University Professors, 1977.

Sherry, A., and Henson, R. "Conducting and Interpreting Canonical Correlation Analysis in Personality Research: A User-Friendly Primer." *Journal of Personality Assessment,* 2005, *84*(1), 37–48.

Snyder, J., Hyer, P., and McLaughlin, G. "Faculty Salary Equity: Issues and Options." *Research in Higher Education,* 1994, *35*(1), 1–19.

Stevens, J. *Applied Multivariate Statistics for the Social Sciences.* (4th ed.) Mahwah, N.J.: Erlbaum, 2002.

Stewart, K., Dalton, M., Dino, G., and Wilkinson, S. "The Development of Salary Goal Modeling: From Regression Analysis to Value-Based Prescriptive Approach." *Journal of Higher Education,* 1996, *67*(5), 555–576.

Strathman, J. "Consistent Estimation of Faculty Rank Effects in Academic Salary Models." *Research in Higher Education,* 2000, *41*(2), 237–250.

Sun, M. "A Multiple Objective Programming Approach for Determining Faculty Salary Equity Adjustments." *European Journal of Operational Research,* 2002, *138,* 302–319.

Tabachnick, B., and Fidell, L. *Using Multivariate Statistics* (5th ed.) Needham Heights, Mass.: Pearson, Allyn & Bacon, 2007.

Toutkoushian, R. (ed.). *Conducting Salary-Equity Studies: Alternative Approaches to Research.* New Directions for Institutional Research, no. 115, San Francisco: Jossey-Bass, 2002.

Toutkoushian, R., Bellas, M., and Moore, J. "The Interaction Effects of Gender, Race, and Marital Status on Faculty Salaries." *Journal of Higher Education,* 2007, *78*(5), 572–601.

Weistroffer, H., Spinelli, M., Canavos, G., and Fuhs, F. "A Merit Pay Allocation Model for College Faculty Based on Performance Quality and Quantity." *Economics of Education Review,* 2001, *20,* 41–49.

SERGE HERZOG is the director for institutional analysis at the University of Nevada, Reno.

This chapter discusses how one institution uses formula funding to project out revenue for future years that will be generated by the university.

Formula Funding, the Delaware Study, and the University of North Carolina

Sarah D. Carrigan

Public higher education has relied on a variety of funding structures since the 1950s. Layzell (2007) describes five general approaches in contemporary use in the United States. *Incremental (baseline) budgeting* uses the current year budget as the base and then makes adjustments to account for expected changes in activities, revenues, and expenditures in the upcoming year. *Funding formulas and guidelines* rely on mathematical formulas to set funding allocations. *Performance funding* is a manner of formula funding that pegs the level of funding to institutional performance on set indicators. Similarly, *performance contracting* is performance funding tied to future, contracted performance. Finally, a *voucher* system provides stipends directly to state residents who are admitted and enrolled at any state institution. These general approaches to public funding are not mutually exclusive, and states commonly use multiple methods to fully allocate funding to their higher education sectors.

North Carolina uses funding formulas to set revenues for the sixteen campuses of the University of North Carolina (UNC) System and the fifty-eight campuses of the North Carolina Community College System. Formula funding across the system was introduced as part of the establishment of the UNC System through the Higher Education Reorganization Act of 1971. Prior to that time, the set of public senior institutions consisted of a six-campus university and ten additional public senior regional institutions, and each approached the North Carolina General Assembly separately for appropriations. The UNC system's funding model also contains aspects of both

NEW DIRECTIONS FOR INSTITUTIONAL RESEARCH, no. 140, Winter 2008   © Wiley Periodicals, Inc.
Published online in Wiley InterScience (www.interscience.wiley.com) • DOI: 10.1002/ir.270

incremental budgeting and performance contracting. Between 1971 and 1998, the funding formula was based in large part on student full-time-equivalent (FTE) enrollment by residency (in-state or out-of-state) and level (undergraduate or graduate). In 1995 the General Assembly directed the UNC board of governors to "review the equity of the current funding system and propose a system of funding which uses identifiable criteria based on educationally and financially sound principles" (University of North Carolina, 1996). Through this review, the board identified the Delaware Study as a primary source for externally tested costs.

Established in 1994, the National Study of Instructional Costs and Productivity, commonly called the Delaware Study, is a robust data collection of disciplinary costs and faculty classroom productivity. This tool was designed to provide benchmark measures at the program level, "specifically for provosts, deans, and department chairs in understanding the relative positions of their academic units with respect to teaching and scholarly productivity and associated costs" (Middaugh, 2002, p. 39). The longitudinal aspect of this study shows whether productivity and costs to the discipline are stable or shift among peers over time.

The Delaware Study has established clear definitions and reporting guidelines for the various data it collects. The study provides four general types of data for each academic department of the institution: academic discipline, degree offerings, fall semester instructional workload, and fiscal year total student credit hour and direct expenditure data. Each academic department is reported by its Classification of Instructional Programs (CIP) discipline, preferably at the four-digit CIP code level, which allows discrete disciplines within broader curricular fields (Middaugh, 1994). For instance, while the general (two-digit) category of social sciences is CIP 45, the four-digit CIP codes for Anthropology and Sociology are 45.02 and 45.11, respectively. Second, the three-year average of degrees awarded is reported at each degree level (bachelor's, master's, doctorate, or first professional). Fall semester instructional workload is reported at the most detailed level, in a four-by-eleven cell grid. Four categories of general faculty make up the grid rows, while the columns indicate faculty total FTE and separately budgeted FTE; student credit hours taught in lower division, upper division, and graduate semester credit hours (SCH); and organized class sections (OCS) by the same division breaks. Academic year SCHs are reported by undergraduate and graduate totals. Finally, fiscal year direct expenditures are reported for salaries, benefits, and other-than-personnel paid from the department's instructional budget, while separately budgeted research and public service expenditures are reported as the final two data points for each department. Middaugh writes:

> Direct expenditure data reflect costs incurred for personnel compensation, supplies, and services used in the conduct of each of these functional areas. They include acquisition costs of capital assets such as equipment and library

books to the extent that funds are budgeted for and used by operating departments for instruction, research, and public service [and] exclude centrally allocated computing costs and centrally supported computer labs, and graduate student tuition remission and fee waivers [Middaugh, 1994].

For each discipline, the spreadsheet calculates a series of measures and ratios from the raw data. These measures are organized in four general tables: Percent SCH and OCS by Faculty Category Within Course Level; Percent SCH and OCS by Course Level Within Faculty Category; SCH, OCS, and FTE Students per FTE Faculty; and Instructional Cost Ratios. These internal calculations are immediately available to the institution for analysis and reporting. The primary product of the Delaware Study is a set of three distinct series of benchmark data tables, available by discipline. Each set of tables is organized from a primary framework: by Carnegie classification of the institution, by highest degree offered in the discipline, and by the undergraduate/graduate program mix within the discipline. The benchmarks are developed in a two-part process. First, an initial mean is calculated for each measure. Institutional responses that are more than two standard deviations away from the initial mean are removed, and a refined mean is recalculated from the remaining responses. The refined mean sets the national benchmark (Middaugh, 2001). Among the myriad benchmarks available, three have become standard measures within the UNC system: SCH per Faculty FTE, OCS per Faculty FTE, and direct instructional expenditures per SCH.

The Delaware Study's academic program benchmarks provide a rational view of differentiated direct costs and credit hour production on which various decision-making tools can be built. In 1998 the UNC System moved to a budgeting plan built on the Delaware Study cost figures, creating a credit hour cost matrix for establishing budgets at each campus. In 1999 the UNC System required all campuses to participate in the Delaware Study so that UNC activity would fully contribute to the benchmark measures. In 2005 the UNC office updated the costing formula using the most recent direct instructional expenditures per SCH benchmarks released by the Delaware Study.

In conjunction with the system's adoption of program cost data from the Delaware Study, the provost at the University of North Carolina—Greensboro (UNCG) requested a Delaware-based credit hour production report from the institutional research office that would assist him in program planning and budget decision making. Over the course of several years, the institutional research office developed and refined several iterations of the enrollment targets report that allows the reader to view trend data showing academic departments on the campus compared with discipline peers for faculty FTE, SCH production, and SCH/FTE. This report is one among several measures used to demonstrate how and to what extent the college or school is meeting institutional priorities, identify programs within the unit that may be overloaded, and justify new faculty lines.

Some departments may be shown to be underserving markets in relation to their discipline peers, suggesting an adjustment to resource allocation and faculty deployment in the classroom is needed. In addition to this campus-level report, the dean of one of the colleges requested a similar report for use in his academic department program reviews. As one element of the program review, this report demonstrates whether the department has met SCH/FTE goals established at the last review cycle, sets the stage for future goals, and is used to support negotiations between the dean and department head for setting priorities and requesting additional support. This chapter describes the ways in which the Delaware Study data have been expanded into ongoing decision-making tools for budgeting and planning at the system, university, and college levels.

The UNC Funding Matrix

Prior to 1971, each state university in North Carolina dealt directly with the North Carolina General Assembly for appropriations requests. In 1971 legislation was passed that reorganized the various public senior higher education institutions into the University of North Carolina. A single entity, the board of governors, was created with the purpose of developing and presenting a comprehensive budget request on behalf of the university. The statutes prescribe that the budget requests are to be presented to the General Assembly in three general categories:

1. Funds for the continuing operation of each constituent institution
2. Funds for salary increases for employees exempt from the state personnel act
3. Funds requested without reference to constituent institutions, itemized as to priority and covering such areas as new programs and activities, expansions of programs and activities, increases in enrollments, increases to accommodate internal shifts and categories of persons served, capital improvements, improvements in levels of operation and increases to remedy deficiencies, as well as other areas (University of North Carolina, 1999a)

Between 1971 and 1998, the continuation budget was designed around a formula driven by student FTE enrollment change. In 1998 the board of governors adopted the SCH Funding Model for Enrollment Change following completion of a study directed by the North Carolina State Legislature in 1995. The purpose of the model is to fund operational requirements based on projected enrollment change measured in SCHs. The funding model is designed to preserve the autonomy of institutions and is used by the UNC General Administration to request and allocate funds to each campus but not to prescribe how the funds are to be used or allocated within the campus administrative structure (University of North Carolina, 1999b).

NEW DIRECTIONS FOR INSTITUTIONAL RESEARCH • DOI: 10.1002/ir

The SCH funding formula addresses five cost components: instructional salary, other academic costs within academic units, library, general institutional support, and financial aid for state residents. It is driven by the projected changes in SCH production in a twelve-cell matrix, defined by four discipline cost categories and three instructional levels (undergraduate, master's, and doctoral).

Instructional position cost factors were first developed using the benchmarks produced from the 1996 National Study of Instructional Cost and Productivity (University of Delaware, 1996) using the cost per credit hour by discipline and Carnegie classification. A UNC-weighted average "was calculated for each discipline by using as weights the percent of fundable UNC total credit hours in that discipline that were offered by each Carnegie category of UNC institutions" (Barnes, 1997, p. 1). Natural break points between the ordered weights were identified to group the complete range of disciplines in the UNC system into four broad cost levels. In the lowest cost category were English, social sciences, mathematics, and philosophy. Cost level II contains education, business, foreign languages and literatures, parks, recreation and fitness, and family and consumer sciences. Biological and physical sciences, computer and information sciences, and visual and performing arts fall into cost category III, and engineering and nursing make up the highest cost category. A weighted average cost was calculated within each level.

Although the Delaware Study cost data are not broken down by course level, the UNC General Administration established relative weightings across course levels using system-specific average class sizes within each cost level, deriving twelve cost factors for the formula. Dividing the change in SCH in each cell by its corresponding weight and then summing the products yields the number of instructional faculty positions required to support the change in SCH. Table 5.1 illustrates the change model for a fictional campus in academic year 2106–2107. The first column on the left lists the four cost levels. The next three columns identify the course level. As a change model, this set of cells shows the difference between the budgeted SCHs and the projected SCHs. In some cells, a positive change has been projected, indicating overall growth expected in the programs that contribute to the given cell. Negative change indicates an expected decline in enrollment compared to the prior budgeted year. The middle three columns list the cost factor associated with each course and cost level. The last three columns on the right list the instructional positions required to support the change in each cell. Below the matrix, the net positions required at each level are summed. For example, the matrix shows that 59.96 faculty FTE would be needed for doctoral instruction. The product of positions required and instructional salary rate (exclusive to each campus) establishes a total instructional salary amount. Additional rates for other academic costs, library, and general institutional support are factored against the instructional salary to arrive at the total requirements to fund the projected enrollment change. Within the framework of the projections formula,

Table 5.1. 2106-07 Request for Enrollment Change

Program Category	Student Credit Hours			SCH per Instructional Position			Instructional Positions Required		
	Undergrad	Masters	Doctoral	Undergrad	Masters	Doctoral	Undergrad	Masters	Doctoral
Category I	1,265	−1,175	746	708.64	169.52	115.56	1.785	−6.931	6.456
Category II	8,446	−18	1,167	535.74	303.93	110.16	15.765	−0.059	10.594
Category III	7,104	525	325	406.25	186.23	109.86	17.487	2.819	2.958
Category IV	512	353	240	232.25	90.17	80.91	2.205	3.915	2.966
	17.327	−315	2,478				37.242	−0.256	59.960
	88.9%	−1.5%	12.7%						
	19.490				Total Positions Required				59.960

student FTEs are also projected, allowing total expected tuition revenue to be projected. This revenue source is subtracted from the total requirements to set the request amount that will be rolled up at the UNC system office into the general budget request submitted to the North Carolina legislature.

The enrollment change model assumes that the current budget adequately supports current enrollments and therefore acts as the base budget. A separate special provision of the General Assembly's 1995 directive was made to conduct a funding equity study. This study resulted in identifying "the need for $21 million in funding equity adjustments for five universities" (University of North Carolina, 1999b). This finding resulted in a $21 million addition to state appropriations for the five identified institutions, effective fiscal year 1997–1998. Changes in the enrollment base drive changes to an institution's budget by adding dollars to support the additional students. By projecting separate enrollment changes within each of the twelve cells of the funding matrix, programmatic changes can be addressed to a finer degree than without disaggregation. Each campus in the UNC system has developed procedures and formulas to future enrollment in both head count and SCHs, grouped in the twelve-cell model of the enrollment change model.

SCH Projections and Enrollment Change Funding at the Campus Level

The process for projecting enrollment at UNCG has features of both centralized and decentralized effort. Three basic components of student enrollment are treated separately: campus-based undergraduate enrollment, campus-based graduate enrollment, and total distance education. Campus-based undergraduate enrollment represents the largest portion of both student head count (74 percent) and credit hour production (83 percent), with stable patterns of enrollment in student classes. This stability and mass allow a centralized approach to projecting future enrollment. The institutional research office has developed a mathematical matrix formula using a Markov chain to model student enrollment patterns. A Markov chain calculates the transitional probabilities for changing from the current category to each possible category. Categories might be defined by student class, status as a full-time or part-time student, major, or other combinations of distinct group identifiers. The matrix allows an estimate of the campus-based undergraduate head count enrollment for any given number of terms into the future by applying prior term transition probabilities to current term enrollments with categorical classes. In addition to projecting student head count enrollment, this formula can be used to project student credit hour enrollment. The average student credit hours carried by students in each cell of the cost matrix is multiplied by the head count enrollment projected for the subsequent term. The sum of these products results in total projected enrollment in the cost matrix, and the difference between projected and budgeted enrollment sets the enrollment change within the cost matrix.

NEW DIRECTIONS FOR INSTITUTIONAL RESEARCH • DOI: 10.1002/ir

Campus-based graduate enrollment accounts for 18 percent of head count and 14 percent of SCH production, and distance education comprises only 8 percent of head count and 3 percent of SCH production. In both cases, with student enrollment highly dependent on small programs, administrative staff members in the Graduate School and Division of Continual Learning work with deans and department heads to estimate enrollment and credit hour production on a program-by-program basis. The sum of all three estimates provides the enrollment projection for the next year in a given enrollment projection cycle. The difference between the projected and the budgeted enrollment establishes the required budget change for the following year.

UNCG has been participating in the Delaware Study since its inception and has assembled a rich database of classroom productivity and comparable Delaware Study norms. The former provost at UNCG chose to use this information to assist in his planning and decision making for allocation of new faculty lines that were budgeted in the enrollment change model. Staff in the institutional research office developed a report that uses the Delaware Study SCH/FTE norms to show historical trends and allow planning and goal setting in the enrollment targets report.

The Delaware Study provides normative data from three perspectives: by Carnegie class of the institution, highest degree awarded within the discipline, and the undergraduate program mix evident in the percentage of undergraduate degrees to total degrees awarded by the program. UNCG has chosen the highest degree awarded as the preferred norm for internal program evaluation. This norm allows the largest potential peer group for comparison at the discipline level and matches for similar program mission across institutions.

In a single page for each academic department, the enrollment targets report (Table 5.2) illustrates trends in faculty FTE, SCH productions, SCH/FTE, and the discipline measured norms at the mean, median, and seventy-fifth percentile. The report calculates a three-year average for each measure and projects productivity targets both in faculty FTE and credit hours for the department to achieve either the mean, median, or seventy-fifth percentile of the three-year average. Using this rich source of data, the provost can immediately identify programs that are performing consistently relative to both their own historic activity and their program peers. The provost then works with each dean to allocate funds to support or enhance academic programs at demonstrated levels of need.

Setting Enrollment Targets

The enrollment targets report (Table 5.2) demonstrates the SCH/FTE trends for the Department of Underwater Basketweaving for the period fall 2003 through fall 2006. The Delaware Study normative data for the CIP category in which Underwater Basketweaving is listed (00.00) are displayed in columns for falls 2003, 2004, and 2005. In each major column section are two subheadings, "Del Norm" and "Target SCH." The Del Norm columns

Table 5.2. Enrollment Targets Report

2007 Enrollment/Credit Hour Production Targets

Department	2003 Del Norm	2003 Target SCH	2004 Del Norm	2004 Target SCH	2005 Del Norm	2005 Target SCH	Three Year Average Del Norm	Three Year Average Target SCH	SCH/FTE	2006 Target SCE	2006 Faculty FTE Production	2007 SCH/FTE Target	2007 Target SCH	2007 Faculty FTE Production
Underwater Basketweaving														
75th Percentile	282.0	2,419.6	363.0	2,631.8	362.0	3,439.0	335.7	2,830.1		3,188.8	11.2			
50th Percentile	252.0	2,162.2	286.0	2,073.5	289.0	2,745.5	275.7	2,327.1		2,618.8	13.6			
Delaware Mean	244.0	2,093.5	292.0	2,117.0	294.0	2,793.0	276.7	2,334.5		2,628.3	13.5			
UNCG SCH/FTE	264.5		329.8		315.5		303.2		394.0					
UNCG-SCH		2,269.0		2,391.0		2,997.0		2,552.3	3,743.0					
UNCG Faculty FTE	8.6		7.3		9.5		8.4		9.5					

Is Underwater Basketweaving performing at or above the mean, fiftieth percentile, or seventy-fifth percentile on credit hour production? Compare fall 2007 UNCG SCH, 3,783, to the three target SCH values shaded in dark gray. The target SCHs compute the number of credit hours that Underwater Basketweaving's eleven faculty FTE would have produced at each normative level. It is preferable to be at or higher than the mean and fiftieth percentile target SCHs.

Is Underwater Basketweaving's faculty FTE comparable to the mean, fiftieth percentile, or seventy-fifth percentile faculty FTE? Compare fall 2007 UNCG faculty FTE, 11, to the three faculty FTE production values, shaded in light gray. The faculty FTE production values compute the FTE that would have produced Underwater Basketweaving's 3,783 SCH at each normative level. It is preferable to be at or smaller than the mean and fiftieth percentile FTEs.

list the norms and the department's actual faculty FTE, SCH, and SCH/FTE. The Target SCH column demonstrates the SCH value that would have been produced by the actual faculty FTE at each normative level. In fall 2003, Underwater Basketweaving had 8.6 FTE faculty and produced 2,269 SCHs. If the department had been performing at the Delaware Study seventy-fifth percentile norm, its 8.6 FTE would have produced 2,420 SCHs.

The middle column in the enrollment targets report produces a three-year average for both the Delaware Study norms and the department's FTE and SCH production. The use of a three-year moving average smoothes out the variance from year to year and provides a stable rate to project goal or target activity, driving the values displayed in the next set of columns to the right to fall 2006. With the Delaware Study norms lagging a year behind the latest department fall production, administrators cannot know how the most current data at the institution would compare to those of peer institutions. The three-year moving average projects what-if scenarios against both actual faculty FTE and actual SCH production. Table 5.2 indicates that in fall 2006, Underwater Basketweaving had 9.5 faculty FTE who produced 3,743 SCHs. From these data, target SCHs are generated by multiplying actual FTE with each of the three-year average norms: mean, median, and the seventy-fifth percentile. In addition, a new subcolumn is added: "Faculty FTE Production." This column postulates the number of faculty who would have produced the department's actual 3,743 SCHs at each of the three-year-average normative levels. The final column, 2007, is left blank to allow work space for setting goals for the upcoming term for both faculty FTE and overall SCH production. Beneath the enrollment targets data are two personalized paragraphs that discuss the relationship between actual SCH and FTE, the norm averages, and the target production.

Given that this report contributes to decision making for academic funding in the following year, it is important for the department to demonstrate that its SCH productivity is at or above the relevant norm. Departments that can demonstrate productivity above the seventy-fifth percentile may be prioritized for additional resources beyond current budget levels.

The Department Review

In addition to the enrollment targets report developed with and for the provost, other reports using data from the Delaware Study have been designed in collaboration with academic deans. The dean of the College of Arts and Sciences needed information to supplement the annual reviews he conducts on a rotating basis with four to six of his departments. These Delaware Study trend reports differ from the enrollment targets report in several ways: the department review shows a five-year rather than three-year trend; only actual productivity figures (no targets) are displayed; and in addition to a table, the data are illustrated with a line graph (Figure 5.1). A second version of this report presents actual data and norms in tabular form

Figure 5.1. Academic Department Review: Credit Hours per Faculty FTE

Delaware Study Trend Report:
Home Department SCH/FTE Compared with
Five Year Norms

Underwater Basketweaving 00.00 (B)	Fall 2001	Fall 2002	Fall 2003	Fall 2004	Fall 2005	Fall 2006
75th Percentile	350.0	319.0	282.0	363.0	362.0	
50th Percentile	259.0	250.0	252.0	286.0	289.0	
Delaware Mean	282.0	270.0	244.0	292.0	294.0	
UNCG SCH/FTE	269.0	268.8	264.5	329.8	315.5	394.0
UNCG SCH	2,098.0	2,486.0	2,269.0	2,391.0	2,997.0	3,743.0
UNCG Faculty FTE	7.8	9.3	8.6	7.3	9.5	9.5

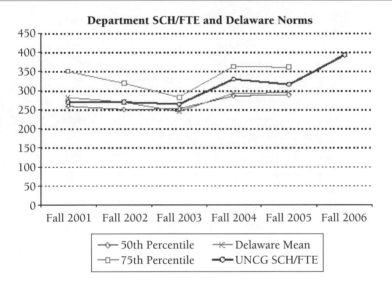

but graphs department data against a five-year average of Delaware norms (Figure 5.2). The report lists both the CIP code (00.00) and the degree level (B, for bachelor) of the norms used for this academic department.

The graph in Figure 5.1 shows Underwater Basketweaving performing solidly between the mean and the seventy-fifth percentile in each year between 2001 and 2005. The fall 2006 SCH/FTE shows a demonstrable jump above the seventy-fifth percentile line, suggesting this department may have made some effort to improve its productivity in the most recent year.

Figure 5.2. Academic Department Review: Credit Hours per Faculty FTE Average Norms

Delaware Study Trend Report:
Home Department Compared with
Five Year Average Norms

Underwater Basketweaving 00.00 (B)	Fall 2001	Fall 2002	Fall 2003	Fall 2004	Fall 2005	Fall 2006
75th Percentile	350.0	319.0	282.0	363.0	362.0	
50th Percentile	259.0	250.0	252.0	286.0	289.0	
Delaware Mean	282.0	270.0	244.0	292.0	294.0	
UNCG SCH/FTE	269.0	268.8	264.5	329.8	315.5	394.0
UNCG SCH	2,098.0	2,486.0	2,269.0	2,391.0	2,997.0	3,743.0
UNCG Faculty FTE	7.8	9.3	8.6	7.3	9.5	9.5

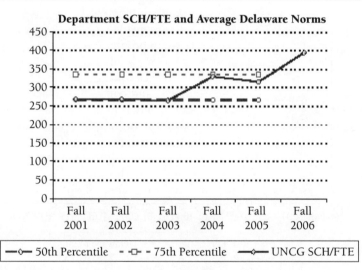

This chart presents percentile figures that are averaged across the past five cycles.

One limitation in this model is the moving target established in each new cycle due to changes in both performance by the peer institutions and peer group membership as institutions join or decline participation in the Delaware Study each year. Figure 5.2 addresses this weakness by smoothing the lines for the mean and the seventy-fifth percentiles with a five-year moving average of each measure. This alternate view suggests that this department's efforts to improve began two years earlier, when productivity moved up from the mean for the first three years, to near the seventy-fifth percentile in the last two years.

NEW DIRECTIONS FOR INSTITUTIONAL RESEARCH • DOI: 10.1002/ir

In addition to reviewing these reports that supplement the department review, the dean has a need to understand the relationship between productivity at the current degree level and the next higher level for departments that are preparing to move up a degree level (such as from offering the master's degree to offering the doctoral degree). UNCG is putting great effort into increasing its research activities, including adding new doctoral degrees to many departments that previously offered only undergraduate and master's degrees. A doctoral-level report alongside the master's-level version allows the dean and department head to set goals with this transition in mind.

Conclusion

This chapter has briefly described how the Delaware Study has been incorporated into administrative decision making at different levels by the University of North Carolina. The Delaware Study was originally designed for provosts, deans, and academic department heads for rational appraisal and planning for academic programs relative to program peers. It has been used for budget formula funding in the University of North Carolina system, determining funding allocations at a single campus from the central administrative unit to academic deans' budgets, and conducting department and program performance reviews. The intent here is to demonstrate current use of this data set in academic budgets and planning. We have found that at the system level, these measures allow rational, performance-based decision making for systemwide budget requests and allocations. At the campus level, these tools are used in conjunction with other measures and data (including research efforts and contract and grants activities) to reveal efficiency and plan future effectiveness of programs or departments.

References

Barnes, G. "Productivity Matrix/SCH Projections. Memo to University of North Carolina Chancellors." Chapel Hill: University of North Carolina, 1997.

Layzell, D. "State Higher Education Funding Models: An Assessment of Current and Emerging Approaches." *Journal of Education Finance,* 2007, 33(1), 1–19.

Middaugh, M. "National Cost Study: Definitions and Terms." 1994. Retrieved Mar. 3, 2008, from http://www.udel.edu/IR/cost/definitions.html.

Middaugh, M. *Understanding Faculty Productivity: Standards and Benchmarks for Colleges and Universities.* San Francisco: Jossey-Bass, 2001.

Middaugh, M. "Faculty Productivity: Different Strategies for Different Audiences." *Planning for Higher Education,* 2002, 30(3), 34–43.

University of Delaware. "1996 National Study of Instructional Cost and Productivity." Newark: University of Delaware, 1996.

University of North Carolina. "UNC Board of Governors Meeting Minutes April 12 1996." Chapel Hill: University of North Carolina, 1996. Retrieved Mar. 17, 2008, from http://www.ga.unc.edu/BOG/minutes/1996/1996_04.pdf.

University of North Carolina. "The University of North Carolina Budget Process."
    Chapel Hill: University of North Carolina, 1999a. Retrieved Feb. 27, 2008, from
    http://ire.uncg.edu/pages/references/BudgetProcess.pdf.
University of North Carolina. "User Manual: University of North Carolina Student Credit
    Hour Enrollment Change Funding Model." Chapel Hill: University of North Carolina,
    1999b. Retrieved Feb. 27, 2008, from http://ire.uncg.edu/pages/references/Funding-
    Manual.pdf.

*SARAH D. CARRIGAN is the assistant vice chancellor and director of institutional
research for the University of North Carolina at Greensboro.*

NEW DIRECTIONS FOR INSTITUTIONAL RESEARCH • DOI: 10.1002/ir

6

This chapter provides an overview of the Kentucky Educational Excellence Scholarship and describes the methodologies and data sources used to derive the biennial state budget projections of student use and costs of the program to the commonwealth.

Budgeting for the Kentucky Educational Excellence Scholarship

Melvin E. Letteer

Kentucky governor Paul Patton, first elected in 1995, came to office with a plan called "Education Pays." The governor recognized from his first days in statewide office as lieutenant governor, simultaneously heading the Economic Development Cabinet, that education is the cornerstone of Kentucky's future. The Kentucky General Assembly in 1998 was poised to pursue a legislative agenda that would significantly increase state funding for postsecondary student financial aid by statutorily designating revenue to the program from the Kentucky state lottery, which began operations in April 1989. Senate Bill 21 was prefiled prior to the 1998 legislative session and began with the following statement of legislative intent:

> The General Assembly of the Commonwealth of Kentucky hereby declares that the best interest of the Commonwealth mandates that financial assistance be provided to ensure access of Kentucky citizens to public and private postsecondary education at the postsecondary educational institutions of the Commonwealth. It is the intent and purpose of the General Assembly that the enactment of [these statutes] shall be construed as a long-term financial commitment to postsecondary education and that the funding provided . . . shall not be diverted from the purposes described in [these statutes] [Kentucky Revised Statutes sec. 164.7871].

New Directions for Institutional Research, no. 140, Winter 2008 © Wiley Periodicals, Inc.
Published online in Wiley InterScience (www.interscience.wiley.com) • DOI: 10.1002/ir.271

The statutes that Senate Bill 21 proposed and were eventually enacted apportioned all of the net revenue from the Kentucky state lottery among three education programs. The statutes require an annual $3 million appropriation to be dispersed to two state-funded adult literacy programs previously funded from general revenue. A second directed appropriation requires 55 percent of the remaining net lottery revenue to be dispersed to the state's two largest need-based postsecondary student financial aid programs: the College Access Program (CAP) and the Kentucky Tuition Grant (KTG) program. After being phased in over a six-year period and becoming fully implemented in academic year 2005–2006, the new funding more than tripled disbursements for need-based aid recipients between fiscal years 1998 and 2007. The third mandatory appropriation dedicates the remaining 45 percent of net lottery revenue be dispersed to the Kentucky Educational Excellence Scholarship (KEES), a merit-based scholarship program created by the legislation.

KEES is a broad-based initiative that provides the opportunity for traditional and nontraditional secondary school students and General Educational Development (GED) recipients to earn scholarships that may be used at Kentucky colleges, universities, and selected technical and vocational education schools in the state. KEES scholarships are used in addition to any need-based student financial aid for which students may otherwise be eligible and does not affect eligibility or the amount of grant aid awarded by those programs. More than one in four KEES recipients in academic years 2004–2005 through 2006–2007 received a CAP or a KTG grant, or both, in addition to their KEES award.

Kentucky Educational Excellence Scholarship

Kentucky legislators had the benefit of observing other states' policies and priorities as they had implemented merit-based scholarship programs. KEES was designed with an understanding that a single point evaluation of high school students or a high-stakes examination to determine merit scholarships lacked the capability to provide a significant educational incentive for most high school students. While the Kentucky Higher Education Assistance Authority (KHEAA) is involved with postsecondary outreach and planning activities for students as young as fourth grade, the first universal direct communication with a student cohort and their parents regarding KEES occurs when Kentucky students complete the eighth grade. KHEAA mails to the home of each student a formal letter over a facsimile of the governor's signature commending the student for his or her educational achievements to date. These letters go on to inform students about the KEES program, as well as other postsecondary financial aid options, and urges consideration of various alternative postsecondary education strategies in conjunction with career aspirations. These letters also direct the students to KHEAA's GoHigher Web site from which students may securely log in and verify their earned KEES awards and access other resources relating to career

NEW DIRECTIONS FOR INSTITUTIONAL RESEARCH • DOI: 10.1002/ir

Table 6.1. KEES Base and Bonus Award Schedule

GPA Range	Base Award	ACT Score	Bonus Award
2.50–2.59	$125	15	$36
2.60–2.69	150	16	71
2.70–2.74	175	17	107
2.75–2.79	187	18	143
2.80–2.89	200	19	179
2.90–2.99	225	20	214
3.00–3.09	250	21	250
3.10–3.19	275	22	286
3.20–3.24	300	23	321
3.25–3.29	312	24	357
3.30–3.39	325	25	393
3.40–3.49	350	26	428
3.50–3.59	375	27	464
3.60–3.69	400	28+	500
3.70–3.74	425		
3.75–3.79	437		
3.80–3.89	450		
3.90–3.99	475		
4.00+	500		

planning and appropriate postsecondary education choices. KHEAA continues these home-oriented communication events annually throughout students' high school years, endeavoring to reinforce the perception among high school students and their parents that all students are expected to pursue some type of postsecondary education or training.

KEES Eligibility

A KEES award has two components, each earned on a sliding-scale: base awards and bonus awards (Table 6.1). Base awards are determined by students' grade point average (GPA) for the academic year at the end of each year. Students may earn up to four base awards—one for each year of high school. Bonus awards are based on the highest reported ACT or ACT-equivalent SAT score a student earned prior to graduation from high school. A minimum of one base award must be earned by traditional high school students before the bonus award may be included in the total KEES award.

Traditional high school students are defined as those who attend a Kentucky Department of Education (KDE) accredited public, private, or parochial high school. Exceptions to this rule are made for high school students attending Congressional Page School and students of active-duty military personnel parents attending Department of Defense high schools.

NEW DIRECTIONS FOR INSTITUTIONAL RESEARCH • DOI: 10.1002/ir

Nontraditional or home-schooled students and GED recipients are pre-cluded by statute from earning KEES base awards but are eligible to earn and use KEES bonus awards. Traditional high school students must take the precollege curriculum defined in regulation by the Kentucky Council on Postsecondary Education (CPE) in order to be eligible for KEES (Kentucky Administrative Regulation 13 KAR 2:020). The precollege curriculum is composed of a minimum of twenty-two units of instruction:

English: four units
Mathematics: three units
Science: three units
Social science: three units
Foreign language: two units
Art/humanities: one unit
Health/physical education: one unit
Electives: five units

Advanced Placement or International Baccalaureate courses may be used to fulfill the requirements in the respective subject areas. Elective courses must be of a level of rigor equal to or greater than that of required courses and must be in the same subject areas as required courses (elective health/physical education may constitute a maximum of one elective unit for the precollege curriculum).

KEES Awards

Students eligible for KEES are any "citizen, national, or permanent resident of the United States and Kentucky resident" attending eligible high schools in Kentucky and taking the precollege curriculum. Students earning a 2.50 GPA or higher at the end of each academic year in high school earn a KEES base award according the sliding-scale schedule in Table 6.1. Base awards accumu-late over the course of a student's high school career, and the maximum KEES base award a student may earn is two thousand dollars (4 – $500).

High school students may also earn a bonus award determined by the highest score that they receive on the ACT or SAT exam. Bonus awards are based on a sliding scale from thirty-six dollars to five hundred dollars (see Table 6.1). The maximum total KEES scholarship high school students may earn is twenty-five hundred dollars in KEES base and bonus awards. This amount is then available to the student for each year of postsecondary study up to four undergraduate years, meaning that an annual twenty-five hundred dollars KEES award may potentially be worth a total of ten thousand dollars. The historical data show that between 2003 and 2007, the average earned KEES scholarship for the more than forty-one thousand traditional high school graduates per year has been approximately twelve hundred dollars.

NEW DIRECTIONS FOR INSTITUTIONAL RESEARCH • DOI: 10.1002/ir

KEES Utilization

The KEES program recognizes that not all students aspire to attain a traditional college or university education at a public university. Therefore, students may use KEES scholarships to attend private universities, community colleges, technical colleges, and most of Kentucky's Title IV–eligible proprietary vocational and technical institutions. Proprietary vocational and technical schools may be considered KEES-eligible institutions if the institution is Title IV eligible and the program of study is at least two years in duration, leading to a certificate, diploma, or degree. This breadth of the postsecondary educational and career training options under KEES has significantly helped Kentucky's high school graduates seek out personally compatible educational choices that they feel will best enhance their future employment opportunities.

Earned KEES scholarships are available to students for up to five years after high school graduation and for up to eight semesters of postsecondary study. Full-time enrollment (twelve or more credit hours per semester) is required for a student to receive full KEES scholarships. The scholarships are proportionately reduced for less than full time but at least half-time enrollment during any semester. The part-time semesters are deducted from the student's overall number of KEES-eligible semesters regardless of the amount disbursed. Students taking less than six hours per semester do not receive any portion of their earned KEES; however, this enrollment does not count against the students' number of semesters of eligibility to receive KEES.

A minimum cumulative GPA requirement is also required for students using KEES scholarships. Recipients must have a minimum 2.50 GPA at the end of the spring semester of their first year of KEES use in order to retain the scholarship for the subsequent academic year. At the end of each spring semester thereafter, KEES recipients must attain a cumulative GPA of 3.00 or higher to retain their full KEES scholarship. A student earning a cumulative GPA between 2.50 and 3.00 results in the student's KEES scholarship being reduced by half. A student may lose KEES for the following year if the cumulative GPA at the end of any spring semester is below 2.50. However, once having lost KEES or having KEES reduced due to a low GPA, a student may regain the KEES scholarship in a subsequent academic year at the appropriate level once his or her cumulative GPA meets or exceeds the 2.50 and 3.00 thresholds.

Utilization of KEES scholarships from the student's perspective is completely paperless. KHEAA pays the scholarship amounts directly to the student's institution through an electronic funds transfer each semester. Postsecondary institutions are required to notify KHEAA each semester that a KEES-eligible student enrolls in courses. Institutions have secure electronic access to KHEAA's student eligibility records in order to verify the KEES scholarship amount and eligibility status of individual students enrolled or accepted for enrollment. Once the institution informs KHEAA of the student's matriculation, KHEAA electronically transfers the student's KEES scholarship for the semester to the institution.

NEW DIRECTIONS FOR INSTITUTIONAL RESEARCH • DOI: 10.1002/ir

KEES Data

The Kentucky Higher Education Assistance Authority (KHEAA) is the state agency charged with the administration of the majority of the state's post-secondary student financial aid programs, the largest of which are the three lottery-funded programs: KEES, CAP, and KTG. Administration of the KEES program necessitates that KHEAA receive, store, and process data that may be conceptually divided into two types: KEES eligibility data and KEES disbursement data. All electronic transfers with KHEAA, regardless of the source or destination of the data, are conducted over secure electronic links. Although KHEAA maintains the capability to process data manually in hard-copy format, all routine data transfers and the vast majority of exception data are accomplished electronically using the secure links.

KEES eligibility data are subdivided into two categories that reflect the two types of KEES awards students may earn: base awards determined by high school GPA and bonus awards determined by ACT or SAT test scores. An ini-tial KEES record originates at the end of the student's eighth-grade year when KHEAA receives students' basic demographic information used to create stu-dent accounts. These accounts are credited with base scholarships as high school GPAs are reported at the end of the students' ninth grade and subse-quent high school years. Public, private, and parochial secondary schools send this information to KHEAA. Data pertaining to student scores on the ACT and SAT tests are received directly from their parent organizations and are used to determine the amount of KEES bonus awards credited to students' accounts.

The general category of KEES disbursement data includes the informa-tion that postsecondary education institutions transmit to KHEAA regard-ing the enrollment of students, such as full- or part-time status and annual and cumulative GPAs. KHEAA uses this information to process disburse-ments made on behalf of students to postsecondary institutions to deter-mine students' renewal award amounts, current eligibility status, and remaining semesters of eligibility.

Overview of the KEES Budget Process

Kentucky statutory law regarding state lottery revenue dedicates 45 percent of net revenue, after a $3 million annual allocation to two state literacy pro-grams, to the KEES trust fund. The administrative process used to make these funds available for disbursement as KEES scholarship grants requires KHEAA to project KEES disbursements for the current fiscal year and each fiscal year of the biennium and include those amounts as line items in KHEAA's bien-nial budget request. The budget requests for all state agencies are then com-bined by the governor's office into an executive budget, which is submitted to the General Assembly. The General Assembly debates the budget in the form of an appropriations bill and may alter the governor's proposed spend-ing priorities before passage, subject to a gubernatorial line-item veto.

New Directions for Institutional Research • DOI: 10.1002/ir

Numerous bills pertaining to KEES have been introduced in the legislature since its inception. The preponderance of these bills includes attempts to redefine, and usually expand, program eligibility. Very few bills have proposed increasing KEES funding levels, which have remained constant since the program's inception. Between academic years 1999–2000 and 2007–2008, average full-time undergraduate tuition and fees at Kentucky's public colleges and universities have increased 137 percent, diminishing the postsecondary education purchasing power of KEES by 57.5 percent (Kentucky Council on Postsecondary Education, 2008). Prior to the 2008 legislative session, no legislation modifying KEES had succeeded in being approved by the legislature.

The actual dollar amount of forecast KEES disbursements per academic year as included in the KHEAA budget is arrived at through the interagency KEES Consensus Forecast Group (KCFG). The KCFG includes representatives from KHEAA (finance and administration cabinet), the Council on Postsecondary Education and the Kentucky Department of Education (education cabinet), and the Governor's Office for Policy Research (an agency within the Office of the State Budget Director). The agencies review and reconcile two KEES budget forecasts: one developed by KHEAA and the other by the Governor's Office for Policy Research. Both agencies use the same set of KEES historic data collected by KHEAA.

The KHEAA projection process for KEES begins in the late summer or early fall of even-numbered years. The preponderance of all high schools and postsecondary institutions have completed data submissions to KHEAA for the preceding academic year, which ended on June 30. This date also marks the end of the state's fiscal year. The data are included in the use analyses for deriving projected KEES disbursements for the current fiscal year and next biennium.

Kentucky high schools are required by statute to submit to KHEAA each academic year a list of all high school students and, separately, an annual report of GPAs for each enrolled student. This data set is used to calculate and report to students and parents earned KEES scholarship awards each year. The data also allow KHEAA to track the number of students enrolled in high schools by grade level, and this forms the basis for KEES projections.

Colleges and universities that are eligible to receive KEES funds on behalf of students verify student eligibility electronically by checking KHEAA's secure online KEES information portal. Once fall and spring semester registrations are complete, the postsecondary institutions transfer to KHEAA an electronic roster of KEES-eligible students and the number of enrolled hours for each student. This roster allows KHEAA to calculate the appropriate KEES award for each student and electronically transfer the KEES funds directly to the institution. The KEES process is completely paperless: students simply register for classes at their chosen KEES-eligible institutions, and their KEES money follows them automatically. At the end of the academic year, postsecondary institutions report to KHEAA each

KEES recipient's cumulative BPA from which KHEAA calculates the student's maximum KEES award for the following year and notifies the student.

Forecasting KEES Use

Disbursement projections developed from these data begin with KHEAA organizing the data into high school graduation cohorts, which serve as the units of analysis. Each cohort is tracked forward through time, beginning in high school, with careful analysis of KEES earning rates and average award amounts, postsecondary enrollment rates, retained enrollment, and retained KEES award amounts. As the KEES program reached full implementation in fiscal year 2005, all of these statistics exhibited similar trends. Within the bounds of annual fluctuations in aggregate amounts, largely driven by changes in the number of students per cohort, the trends increased rapidly during the early years in most measures, slowed as the program reached maturity, and currently show very slow growth. Today virtually all relevant measures are increasing slowly and at a decreasing rate. A linear extrapolation of these trends would overestimate actual future values by substantial amounts. Logarithmic trend projections yield much stronger projections of future use.

Annual KEES budget projections are derived from two projected measures for each high school cohort for each postsecondary fiscal year: the number of students likely to attend eligible postsecondary institutions and the expected average amount of their individual KEES awards. The use rates for KEES recipients in each cohort in each year are extrapolated from historical KEES experience as ratios of the number of students likely to attend to the total number of students in the cohort. Similarly, expected average disbursed award amounts are extrapolated from historical data as the ratio of earned KEES awards to the maximum possible KEES award. The first ratio is multiplied by the actual number of students in the original cohort to yield the expected number of students who would receive KEES disbursements in the year. The second ratio is multiplied by the maximum possible KEES award for these students and yields an approximation of the average KEES award to be disbursed to the members of the particular cohort for the year. Multiplying these two numbers yields the expected total disbursement for each cohort during this year. Table 6.2 presents an example of the KHEAA projections for fiscal year 2008, the current year, and the upcoming 2009–2010 biennium.

Table 6.2 shows that 153 students graduated from high school in 2008 and will receive KEES disbursements in fiscal year 2008. Typically these students completed high school in the fall semester of 2007, enrolled in a postsecondary institution in the spring semester of 2008, and are included in the fiscal year 2008 disbursements. It should be noted that KEES awards may not be used for dual-credit or dual-enrollment courses while students are still in high school. KEES may be used only after high school graduation and may not be used for postsecondary summer term enrollment.

NEW DIRECTIONS FOR INSTITUTIONAL RESEARCH • DOI: 10.1002/ir

Table 6.2. KEES Projected Disbursements, Fiscal Years 2008–2010

High School Graduation Cohort	FY 2008		FY 2009		FY 2010	
	Students	Awards	Students	Awards	Students	Awards
1999	0	$0	0	$0	0	$0
2000	3	2,691	0	0	0	0
2001	17	16,854	3	3,803	0	0
2002	57	49,059	25	24,851	4	4,870
2003	3,403	2,820,759	61	52,898	33	37,443
2004	11,256	15,858,042	3,316	2,736,256	61	52,591
2005	12,518	17,729,543	11,394	16,066,159	3,343	2,753,022
2006	14,268	22,178,758	12,597	17,877,610	11,461	16,172,817
2007	23,098	31,061,657	14,604	22,753,821	12,909	18,353,869
2008	153	89,382	23,675	31,880,691	14,974	23,377,079
2009	0	0	170	99,251	23,901	32,226,090
2010	0	0	0	0	188	109,195
Total	64,774	$89,806,747	65,845	$91,495,340	66,873	$93,086,976

Source: KHEAA Research and Policy Analysis.

Table 6.2 also shows that a cohort's largest proportional impact on KEES enrollment and disbursement occurs in the first year after the cohort graduates from high school. It diminishes by approximately one-third for the sophomore year of college for every cohort and then declines at a much slower pace through the third and fourth postsecondary years. Table 6.3 presents disbursement percentages for postsecondary academic years for two recent cohorts of high school graduates using KEES in postsecondary education. The cohort's first full year typically consumes slightly more than

Table 6.3. Percentage of KEES Disbursement by Postsecondary Class by Academic Year

Postsecondary Class	2005–2006	2006–2007
First year	34.547%	34.515%
Second year	25.061	24.451
Third year	20.086	19.757
Fourth year	17.762	18.041
Fifth year	2.448	2.942
Sixth year	0.027	0.043
Seventh year	0.002	0.006

Source: KHEAA KEES data extract, Feb. 13, 2008.

NEW DIRECTIONS FOR INSTITUTIONAL RESEARCH • DOI: 10.1002/ir

Table 6.4. Percentage of Postsecondary Enrollment for KEES-Earning High School Graduates by Number of Years After High School Graduation

Graduation Cohort	Academic Years After High School Graduation						
	+1	+2	+3	+4	+5	+6	+7
1999	61.0%	37.8%	32.8%	30.1%	9.3%	0.16%	0.01%
2000	60.6	38.4	33.6	30.7	9.4	0.14	0.04
2001	61.4	39.3	33.7	30.6	9.3	0.16	0.05
2002	61.6	39.1	34.1	31.3	9.1	0.16	(0.07)
2003	59.8	37.9	33.4	30.5	9.1	(0.17)	(0.09)
2004	61.6	38.8	34.1	31.0	(9.1)	(0.17)	(0.11)
2005	61.0	38.3	34.1	(31.0)	(9.1)	(0.17)	(0.13)
2006	61.8	38.7	(34.2)	(31.1)	(9.1)	(0.17)	(0.15)
2007	61.3	(38.7)	(34.2)	(31.1)	(9.0)	(0.18)	(0.17)
2008	(61.3)	(38.8)	(34.3)	(31.1)	(9.0)	(0.18)	(0.19)
2009	(61.3)	(38.8)	(34.4)	(31.2)	(9.0)	(0.18)	(0.21)
2010	(61.3)	(38.8)	(34.4)	(31.3)	(9.0)	(0.19)	(0.23)

Note: Statistics in parentheses are projections.

Source: KHEAA KEES data extract, Feb. 13, 2008.

one-third of total annual KEES disbursements. Cohorts beyond the first year of postsecondary education consume decreasing percentages of total disbursements as students lose their KEES awards due to insufficient grades, reduce their attendance to less than full time, transfer to institutions or programs that are not KEES eligible, or drop out of postsecondary education.

Table 6.4 lists the historical percentages of students for each cohort who were retained and received KEES in each year after high school and the projected percentages. These percentages undercount the true number of Kentucky high school graduates enrolling in postsecondary education by omitting students enrolled at out-of state institutions or institutions that are not Title IV eligible or do not offer academic programs of at least two years' duration or students enrolling for less than six hours per semester.

Typically postsecondary students may use earned KEES awards for eight semesters of study within five years of high school graduation. CPE may designate individual programs of study as five-year undergraduate programs, which extend KEES eligibility for an additional two semesters. Finally, Table 6.4 also shows a very small percentage of individuals using KEES six and seven years after high school graduation, normally beyond a student's statutory KEES eligibility period. The very small percentages in these columns are due to students' having received an extension of KEES eligibility, usually because of military service.

NEW DIRECTIONS FOR INSTITUTIONAL RESEARCH • DOI: 10.1002/ir

Forecasting KEES Award Amounts

KEES earnings rates are initially totaled from the raw data for each cohort, and the average earned KEES award for each cohort of students earning KEES is calculated. In order to be able to use earned KEES awards, traditional high school students must earn at least one base award. Supplemental KEES awards based on ACT or SAT test scores must be earned prior to high school graduation. The latter criterion does not apply to nontraditional high school students (GED recipients and home-schooled students) who are eligible only for KEES supplemental awards. Nontraditional KEES-earning students are assigned to the cohort for the fiscal year in which they receive their GED or diploma.

Table 6.5 presents the earned KEES statistics used in the forecasting process. It shows that more than 85 percent of high school graduates in Kentucky have earned at least one KEES award, and the average KEES award ranges between $1,180 and $1,200. This indicates that the ratio of the average KEES award earned to the maximum possible KEES award for each cohort over the last five years has been relatively stable at approximately 47.7 percent.

The number of students per cohort, the total value of earned KEES awards, and the average earned KEES award grew very rapidly during the first five years of the program as the number of high school students completing with earned KEES increased with each new cohort. This effect was compounded by the fact that the statutory implementation plan for KEES specified a tiered schedule of maximum possible awards for each of the first

Table 6.5. Earned KEES Awards by High School Graduating Cohort

Graduation Cohort	Total High School Graduates	KEES Earning Students	Earned KEES	Maximum Possible	Average	Ratio Average to Maximum
1999	39,235	29,835	$13,229,561	$800	$443	0.554
2000	39,334	32,414	24,535,925	1,500	757	0.505
2001	40,438	34,253	33,112,499	2,000	967	0.483
2002	39,970	35,192	41,702,050	2,500	1,185	0.474
2003	42,768	37,203	43,780,648	2,500	1,177	0.471
2004	41,379	36,285	43,504,815	2,500	1,199	0.480
2005	41,629	36,691	43,811,329	2,500	1,194	0.478
2006	42,122	37,123	44,553,289	2,500	1,200	0.480
2007	43,628	37,741	44,904,798	2,500	1,190	0.476
2008	–	38,629	46,197,897	2,500	1,196	0.478
2009	–	38,987	46,671,116	2,500	1,197	0.479
2010	–	39,314	47,101,939	2,500	1,198	0.479

Note: Statistics from 2008 and onward are projections.

Source: KHEAA KEES data extract, Feb. 13, 2008.

NEW DIRECTIONS FOR INSTITUTIONAL RESEARCH • DOI: 10.1002/ir

Table 6.6. Average KEES Award Used as Percentage of Maximum KEES Award for KEES-Earning High School Graduates Attending Postsecondary Institutions, by Number of Years After High School Graduation

Graduation Cohort	Academic Years Post High School Graduation						
	+1	+2	+3	+4	+5	+6	+7
1999	57.2%	63.4%	57.1%	58.3%	36.5%	41.0%	66.5%
2000	53.6	60.9	55.8	56.4	33.6	34.4	31.7
2001	52.4	59.8	55.1	55.9	33.2	34.5	(49.1)
2002	52.3	60.2	55.3	55.8	32.7	(34.4)	(40.4)
2003	53.2	61.2	55.9	56.3	(33.2)	(34.5)	(44.7)
2004	53.3	61.5	56.3	(56.4)	(33.0)	(34.5)	(42.6)
2005	53.4	61.5	(56.7)	(56.4)	(32.9)	(34.5)	(43.6)
2006	53.5	(62.2)	(56.8)	(56.4)	(33.0)	(34.5)	(43.1)
2007	(53.8)	(62.3)	(56.9)	(56.5)	(33.0)	(34.5)	(43.4)
2008	(53.9)	(62.4)	(57.0)	(56.5)	(33.0)	(34.5)	(43.2)
2009	(53.9)	(62.6)	(57.0)	(56.5)	(33.0)	(34.5)	(43.3)
2010	(54.0)	(62.7)	(57.1)	(56.6)	(33.0)	(34.5)	(43.3)

Note: Statistics in parentheses are projections.

Source: KHEAA KEES data extract, Feb. 13, 2008.

three cohorts before reaching the maximum KEES award of twenty-five hundred dollars with the fourth (2002) graduation cohort.

The average award amounts listed in Table 6.5 are aggregate averages for the cohort. Not all students in a cohort continue on to postsecondary education and the ones who do tend to have higher earned KEES awards. The amount of the average KEES award used changes as cohorts move from one academic class to the next through the postsecondary education system. The result is that there are different ratios of used award amounts to maximum award amounts for each cohort for each academic class, designated as the number of years since high school graduation (see Table 6.6).

Average KEES award amounts used tend to be largest in the sophomore year, at the end of which one-third of KEES users lose their KEES awards due to insufficient grades or do not persist through the sophomore year. Average KEES awards in the junior and senior years are somewhat lower than the sophomore year, as many of the community college students complete their education, with the associate of arts their final degree. Also, many students who have lost their KEES awards in the first two years earn them back in the latter two years. The average KEES award used falls significantly beyond year 4 because a higher percentage of students enroll as part-time students, many with only six credit hours per semester, the minimum required to be eligible to receive a KEES award.

New Directions for Institutional Research • DOI: 10.1002/ir

The data on the number of high school students projected to graduate with earned KEES awards, the extrapolated KEES use patterns of high school graduation cohorts, and the average KEES award used at each postsecondary year of attendance are combined in Table 6.2, which shows KHEAA's KEES forecast for the current fiscal year and the upcoming biennium.

Arriving at the official KEES forecast first requires KHEAA personnel to meet with personnel from the Governor's Office for Policy Research, which also prepared an independent KEES forecast, in order to reconcile any substantive differences between the two agencies' numbers. The individual agency forecasts have always been remarkably close. During the last budget cycle, the differences between the two forecasts were less than one-half of 1 percent for each of fiscal years 2009 and 2010. Agreement is usually reached on a single set of forecasts very quickly.

The final step in formalizing the KEES forecasts is accomplished at a meeting of the KEES Consensus Forecast Group, which consists of members from KHEAA, the Governor's Office for Policy Research, the Office of the State Budget Director, the Council on Postsecondary Education, and the Kentucky Department of Education. Budget analysts from KHEAA and the Governor's Office for Policy Research present the final budget and respond to any questions the panel might have. The panel generally recommends adoption of the forecast as the final KEES projected budget. The final budget is then included in KHEAA's biennial budget request.

Conclusion

The Kentucky Higher Education Assistance Authority, as an agency in the finance and administration cabinet, has two primary functions within the sphere of higher education. First, KHEAA is charged with administering state-sponsored scholarship and grant student financial aid programs, and second, KHEAA is a federal family education loan guarantor. The KEES scholarship program is the second largest student financial aid program in the state in terms of disbursed dollars. KEES is projected to disburse over $90 million in each year of the 2009–2010 biennium in addition to another $105 million in need-based and targeted student financial aid. KHEAA annually publishes aggregate summary data on each program on its Web site (www.kheaa.com). Publication of the annual volumes of the KEES Data Book may be found at that location.

The KEES program disbursed more than $88.5 million in scholarship payments on behalf of postsecondary students during fiscal year 2007 and has made in excess of $453 million in disbursements to college students since the program began. Nonetheless, KEES has been able to remain within the statutory fiscal limit of 45 percent of net lottery revenue. Annual fluctuations in lottery revenue and incremental increases in KEES use over time, however, may at some point raise concern among government officials that the demand for KEES posed by students using earned KEES awards may

NEW DIRECTIONS FOR INSTITUTIONAL RESEARCH • DOI: 10.1002/ir

exceed available dedicated revenue. Were net lottery revenue in any fiscal year to prove insufficient to provide adequate funding for KEES, the disbursement forecasting process through the KEES Consensus Forecast Group would alert members of the executive and legislative branches of this potential situation. While KHEAA possesses the statutory authority to reduce KEES scholarship award payments on behalf of postsecondary students in order to alleviate a structural budgetary imbalance, other policy alternatives would have to be carefully scrutinized.

Reference

Kentucky Administrative Regulation (13 KAR 2:020). "Guidelines for Admission to the State-Supported Postsecondary Institutions in Kentucky." Kentucky Legislative Research Commission, 2008. Retrieved Apr. 29, 2008, from http://www.lrc.ky.gov/kar/013/002/020.htm.

Kentucky Council on Postsecondary Education. "Tuition History, Kentucky Public College and Universities—Full-Time Undergraduate Resident Tuition and Fees." 2008. Retrieved Apr. 29, 2008, from http://cpe.ky.gov/NR/rdonlyres/38C9B1BB-1CA5-4379-AA1C-2015B3B9347D/0/Tuition_History_1987_2009.pdf.

Kentucky Revised Statutes. "Kentucky State Lottery." Kentucky Legislative Research Commission, 2008. Retrieved Apr. 29, 2008, from http://www.lrc.ky.gov/KRS/154A00/CHAPTER.HTM.

Kentucky Revised Statutes. "Kentucky Educational Excellence Scholarship." Kentucky Legislative Research Commission, 2008. Retrieved Apr. 29, 2008, from http://www.lrc.ky.gov/KRS/164-00/CHAPTER.HTM.

MELVIN E. LETTEER is an economist with the Kentucky Higher Education Assistance Authority and the Kentucky Higher Education Student Loan Corporation and leads the Research and Policy Analysis Division.

NEW DIRECTIONS FOR INSTITUTIONAL RESEARCH • DOI: 10.1002/ir

7

This chapter discusses the use of a return on investment models for higher education institutions.

Using Return on Investment Models of Programs and Faculty for Strategic Planning

Lawrence J. Redlinger, Nicolas A. Valcik

Traditional conceptions of faculty and program productivity typically emphasize in varying degrees teaching, research, publication, creative work, service to the university, and service to the community. Evaluation of these areas and the relative weights assigned to them varies greatly from unit to unit within a university and even more so among universities. Moreover, without measurable weights assigned to each activity, it becomes more difficult to make planning decisions ranging from funding new positions to posttenure review of faculty. The lack of data also makes a more objective evaluation of faculty and program performance much less likely. Thus, it is no surprise that decisions about teaching load, class size, curriculum, programs, and faculty appear to be driven more by polemics than by analysis. In truth all faculty activities create value and entail costs for universities. Although we strongly do not believe that all programmatic and faculty activity can be reduced to financial considerations, we also believe that financial considerations must play an important part in evaluating how resources are invested by the university and if those investments are in the best interests of the students, the faculty as a whole and the short- and long-term goals of the university.

The model we discuss here for Texas focuses on the revenue streams and expenditures for different areas of a university, makes use of data routinely available in a university's databases, and takes into account the percentage of

NEW DIRECTIONS FOR INSTITUTIONAL RESEARCH, no. 140, Winter 2008 © Wiley Periodicals, Inc.
Published online in Wiley InterScience (www.interscience.wiley.com) • DOI: 10.1002/ir.272

time to which a faculty member is assigned or is engaged in varied activities. The approach allows unit heads to have a comparative manner in which to track relative performance over time and use this information to make strategic decisions. Coupled with other measures (including teaching evaluations, class dropout rates, and measures of student learning), our "return on investment" (ROI) model creates a more robust means for continued and future allocation of campus resources and establishes the basis for performance evaluation publicly available to all those concerned.

One criticism of this approach arises from the perspective that universities are not businesses, that bodies of knowledge and disciplinary majors are not product lines, and that intellectual workers cannot be evaluated in terms of cost and revenue streams. We believe these are valid concerns lest universities discontinue teaching certain fields of study because they are temporarily unpopular or, however necessary, appear to a given set of students to be too difficult. But colleges and universities that ignore the relationship of revenues to costs do so at their own peril. Tighter analysis of the cost of instruction is being undertaken by many state agencies and used to establish funding formulas. Nationally, the burden for funding higher education has been shifting to students, while at the same time there are greater pressures on institutions of higher education to demonstrate accountability in how they use resources. It may be that schools with large endowments or high demand from students can afford some inefficiencies (even though there is a strong relationship between student subsidies and SAT scores), but in the rich cornucopia that is American higher education, there are many more state and small schools whose continued survival depends on efficient monetary management (Winston, 1997). As one moves down the endowment list from the top one hundred institutions, endowments drop off rather precariously. Many schools do not have sufficient resources to retain programs that cannot provide quality education in a cost-effective, efficient, and learning effective manner.

While we offer no panacea to these problems, we do provide schools with a model and a tool for assessing their strategy in using resources toward the best interests of the students and the effectiveness of organizational stewardship with which they have been entrusted. The results of the modeling provide a common basis for policy discussions of issues that have remained obscured in academe. For example, what is the appropriate compensation for a departmental chair position? What is an appropriate teaching load, and what rewards should be available on a merit basis for those who teach many students and teach them well? Why do some programs that are similar in size and needs cost more than other programs? The comparative data generated by the ROI model allow clarity in these types of policy discussions.

The overall model views students as revenue generators for the university. Outside scholarships, grants, loans, and other forms of subsidy flow through students, who then apply the funds toward tuition to the university and, in our case, generate formula funding. A large portion of the revenue generated by students is allocated to faculty to teach the students. A smaller portion is budgeted for administrative and other instructional costs. The program RETINA (RETurn on INvestment Analysis) focuses on cyclical flows of revenue from student to instructor (stream of costs) and the revenue stream (income) that results with the delivery of instructional services. The instructional services are related to student learning and the course election decisions by students. These course elections produce further income streams for programs. Programs can create demand for a course by declaring it a core or required course as long as there is a sufficient supply of student willing to take the course and program. The relationship comprises a significant portion of the larger cash flow model illustrated in Figure 7.1.

As with any other project, the design of the model is crucial to obtaining accurate results. In Texas, state colleges and universities operate in a formula-funding environment. In this environment, public funds are allocated based on a formula that uses (1) the student's class level (freshmen, sophomore, junior, or senior), (2) the course level (lower, upper, master's, or doctoral) in which the student is enrolled, and (3) the course type (science, engineering, and so on). Depending on the student's class level, the level of the course, and the course type, a "dollar amount" of formula funding per semester credit hour is allocated. Currently the state formula uses five divisions for stratifying course levels: lower division (freshmen and sophomore), upper division (junior and senior), master's, doctoral, and professional. The base credit hour rate is for a lower-division (freshmen or sophomore) student taking a liberal arts course. Liberal arts courses are defined by their CIP designations and include, for example, history, government, and English. There are twenty-one categories (see Table 7.1) ranging across the lower division to doctoral levels. Weights are applied to the base credit hour in the formula depending on various designations of course work and conceptions of the actual costs of instruction in an area. For example, the weight for fine arts master's-level (5.91) is approximately the same as the weight for master's-level instruction in agriculture (7.14) because of the presumed parity in the costs of instruction, overhead, and support. For years the funding matrix logic remained unexamined, with the weights adjusted more or less incrementally. In 2003, a formal review of the underlying structure of the formula was undertaken, and subsequently a separate set of data is now used to determine the weights in the matrix (Redlinger and Gordon, 2005). The dollar amount per base SCH (that the formula is funded [Table 7.1]) is recommended by the coordinating board, but the actual rate is established by the legislature.

The instruction and operations formula relies on the lowest common denominator between the student's status and the course level. For example, a freshman taking a senior-level course receives freshmen funding, and a senior taking a course for freshman receives freshmen funding (see below). The base rate recommended for the 2006–2007 biennium was $55.72. In addition to the instruction and operations formula, there is an infrastructure support formula associated with plant-related formulas and utilities driven by the predicted square feet for universities' educational

Figure 7.1. General Academic Institutions Formula Funding Used for the 2006–2007 Biennium

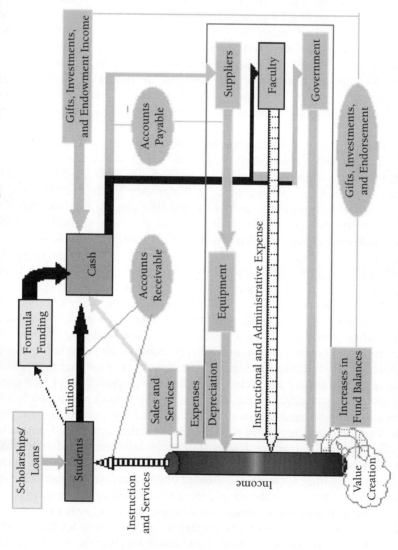

Source: Texas Higher Education Coordinating Board (2008 and adapted from Purcell [1983]).

Table 7.1. General Academic Institutions Formula Funding Used for the 2006–07 Biennium

CIP Code	Lower Division	Upper Division	Master's	Doctoral	Professional
Liberal Arts	1.00	1.86	4.07	10.89	
Science	1.66	3.00	7.63	19.72	
Fine Arts	1.63	2.74	5.91	12.31	
Teacher Education	1.34	1.91	2.89	8.41	
Agriculture	2.06	2.62	7.14	13.43	
Engineering	2.43	3.28	7.21	18.35	
Home Economics	1.32	1.97	3.70	8.47	
Law					3.39
Social Services	2.01	2.30	4.59	12.10	
Library Science	1.28	1.33	3.59	8.85	
Vocational Training	2.14	2.52			
Physical Training	1.35	1.30			
Health Services	2.10	2.80	6.10	12.75	
Pharmacy	2.45	3.39	13.75	22.72	6.37
Business Administration	1.24	1.61	3.95	16.59	
Optometry			5.46	19.12	7.00
Teaching Education Practice	1.75	2.19			
Technology	1.93	2.46	5.59		
Nursing	3.58	4.96	5.89	13.49	
Developmental Education	1.00				
Veterinary Medicine					15.44

Source: Texas Higher Education Coordinating Board, 2008.

and general activities is produced by the space projection model developed by the coordinating board.

Although there have been many criticisms of the formula funding system in Texas, it is in fact the primary method by which the state allocates general appropriations to its public institutions. Obviously in a private school or university not funded by these means, these considerations do not matter. In our case, however, establishing the true reimbursement rate is the first step in creating the measurement of the state revenue stream. In a larger sense, any institution that wishes to accurately track its revenue flow and return on investment can use the concepts and practices presented here.

Table 7.2 provides a hypothetical breakdown of how the current formula funds different portions of the education and general (E&G) budget. The state's coordinating board recommended base formula rate was $55.72. However, the actual rate used by the legislature can be determined only after allocations are made. In this example, the actual funded rate, or de facto rate, is $47.04, or 84.4 percent of the recommended rate. Thus, the base we are using is $47.04. The contribution of the formula to faculty salaries is $34.40, or 73.1 percent. The remainder contributes to library, departmental

NEW DIRECTIONS FOR INSTITUTIONAL RESEARCH • DOI: 10.1002/ir

Table 7.2 State Formula Funding Academic Year 2007–2008

Category	De Facto Rate per Earning Unit[a]
Faculty salaries	$34.40
Departmental operations	6.23
Instructional administration[b]	2.17
Direct research support[c]	1.69
Library	2.56
Total	47.04
Coordinating Board recommended rate	55.72

[a]One unit = one lower-level undergraduate liberal arts hour.
[b]Includes deans' offices and computer support but not the provost office.
[c]Support for research centers.

operations, instructional administration, and research support. So each semester credit hour makes a contribution to all of these areas (Table 7.2).

To obtain a complete picture of revenue flows, additional factors need to be considered. Faculty members engage in activities other than teaching. First, some faculty members work on research projects. This activity, insofar as it is externally funded, is a value-added activity for the university. Moreover, when it is externally funded, the proportion of the faculty member's salary funded by formula is reduced by the amount compensated by the contract or grant. In most cases for federal grants and contracts, the portion of faculty salary paid by the grant or contract reduces the amount of time the faculty member works on state funds. This is not true, for example, for certain types of training grants where the faculty member may administer the grant but the main beneficiaries are graduate students. It is also not true for faculty engaged in research who receive reduced teaching loads but whose activity is paid for out of state funds. A department chair or dean may grant a faculty member reduced course loads to write a grant proposal or finish a book but pay for that reduced load out of state funds. In our model, this subsidy shows up as a deficit since state funds are supporting the activity.

Second, there are faculty members who are either granted or given special assignments. Special assignments are more difficult to assess because they intrude into the system from multiple points. A common pattern in universities is the reduction of teaching load as compensation for undertaking a special assignment such as departmental chair. Alternatively, faculty may be given summer support, in which case their teaching load remains the same during the academic year. In instances where administrative or special assignments are funded out of faculty salary accounts, those faculty often show up as deficits on a basic ROI analysis of revenue generated from teaching activities. There are cost allocation questions related to these types of assignments. For example, departmental chair activities and associated

NEW DIRECTIONS FOR INSTITUTIONAL RESEARCH • DOI: 10.1002/ir

costs are borne generally by the department as a whole in the same way as other departmental operations and support. Costs for special assignments that affect the university as a whole, such as reaccreditation efforts, are distributed more widely. Our approach to these assignments is to embed the costs in university-wide administrative overhead. However, the actual calculations for these types of costs vary from university to university and in some cases are not considered at all.

The next step is to compile a program to report state-funded salaries versus state revenue (as measured by formula funding) generated and to group individuals by school, program or department, and faculty status (tenured professor, tenure-track professor, lecturer, and teaching assistant). These data also allow the grouping of costs and revenues by subject matter, course level, time of offering, and other measures. The resulting data can be analyzed using descriptive statistics and inferential techniques. Over a given time period, such as six semesters or three academic years, trends in performance can be revealed for programs, courses, faculty, and other units of analysis.

RETurn on INvestment Analysis (RETINA): The Program

RETINA is part of a larger database management system that analyzes faculty costs and the flow of instructional resources. There is a collateral management system for the physical plant and inventory. The primary objective of RETINA is to estimate revenues generated by semester and for an academic year. In this respect, RETINA calculates the revenue generated per class according to state formula funding guidelines. With regard to tuition, the calculations have become more complicated over time. Our university has implemented a guaranteed four-year tuition plan for students as well as retaining traditional plans for continuing students. As a result, course enrollments must be disaggregated to the student level to see what tuition plan applies to each student; the data are then reaggregated for the course under question. We have also created a separate program that captures the tuition and fees collected from students and assigns students by the courses in which they are enrolled.

In Texas, statutory (state-established) tuition is collected and transitioned to Austin into the Uniform Statewide Accounting System after which the university is reimbursed for "expenses." Another type of tuition, "designated tuition," is also collected but remains with the university. Ultimately these funds, or portions thereof, show up in the education and general account of the university. The second objective of RETINA is to determine the cost to the university of various forms of work endeavors as measured by salaries paid to faculty members from state accounts. RETINA was modified in 2007 to incorporate staff and faculty salaries extracted directly from the Human Resource System (see Chapter Two for more information on the University of Texas at Dallas's system staff/faculty extract).

NEW DIRECTIONS FOR INSTITUTIONAL RESEARCH • DOI: 10.1002/ir

RETINA uses faculty salary information that is based on dollars actually paid to employees rather than on budgeted salary information to more accurately determine actual costs incurred. RETINA can then be applied toward an ROI calculation to determine efficiencies at the faculty, program of instruction, department, or school levels with greater accuracy. RETINA can also determine revenue and expenditures on specific areas of concern, such as graduate assistants' salaries, whereas a budget file might typically report a single encumbered amount. RETINA can also calculate the relative monetary contributions of revenue from classroom instruction to other areas, such as departmental overhead, staff salaries, and designated fees. However, our purpose in this chapter is to focus on the relationship between instructional costs, as measured by state-funded faculty salaries, formula funding, tuition, and measures of income.

Methodology. There are several limitations of RETINA that must be noted at the onset. First, RETINA does not take into account administrative duties performed by faculty members that are funded using state funds in the instructional budget. For example, if the chair of a department is given a course reduction or summer support by the dean as "payment" for administrative duties, RETINA will not capture this nuance. Instead, RETINA output will show the chair as a deficit to be explained by the dean to the provost. Nonetheless, this output provides a dean or provost with valuable insight into the relative cost of administration per department. If there are two departments of the same size and complexity and two administrative supplements (course reductions) of disproportionate amounts (say, fifteen thousand dollars versus eight thousand dollars), a question arises as to the efficacy of the reward system. In this sense, RETINA provides an alternative basis for examining policy and practice.

A second limitation is that RETINA does not exclude students whose status is such that their semester credit hours do not generate state formula funding. Examples for Texas are undergraduates who have accrued more than 170 semester credit hours and doctoral students whose doctoral credit hours surpass 100 hours. For better or worse, these semester credit hour requirements were set into law by the legislature. We have discussed elsewhere the effects of these requirements in terms of their differential effects on universities, community college transfers, and minority students.

These students are small in number at our university and continue to pay tuition; pragmatically, too, there is not a simple way to differentiate these students in the student system. It is possible after the reporting period in which these students have been identified to remove them for state funding purposes, but they still pay tuition. For our university, the number of students in this situation is so small that the additional refinement is unwarranted.

Furthermore, every legislative session considers or passes modifications to the laws that create these special classes of students. A small population group at the mercy of these legislative winds can safely be excluded in most ROI modeling without adversely affecting data accuracy and the general

NEW DIRECTIONS FOR INSTITUTIONAL RESEARCH • DOI: 10.1002/ir

policymaking of the university. However, changes in residency requirements, for example, must be taken into account because such a change would greatly affect the funding or tuition status of large groups of students.

Third, RETINA excludes nonfunded classes. Classes in this category include all executive education courses in which the students pay a fee that covers, in theory, the full cost of instruction. In virtually all circumstances, faculty members teaching these courses are not supported by state funds but derive their salary from the executive education programs.

Fourth, RETINA does not account for tuition exemptions and waivers. While these amounts are not trivial for our university, they are also not a direct result of the faculty, program, or school effort. Also, exemptions and waivers are determined by student status (scholarship, teaching assistants, or special out-of-state). We assume these situations are distributed across the total credit hour production in a proportional manner. Figure 7.2 summarizes the information that RETINA captures and calculates.

Information for RETINA is taken from Strategic Planning and Analysis files, the HRS, and the Student Information System (SIS+) and merged to obtain results. The first step is to calculate semester credit hours and the value of those hours for each class. In some other university or college systems, this calculation is a simpler task than public higher education institutions in Texas. As noted, semester credit hour revenue values are based on a lowest common denominator formula (using the lowest value of either course level or student level), and thus each set of course hours must be weighted appropriately. Information on the faculty member teaching the class, including salary, is then added to the file in order to charge back the hours to the correct program, department, or school. This step in the process is necessary since some professors teach courses in more than one program and at both the undergraduate and graduate levels.

Figure 7.2. RETINA Program Summary of Calculations

RETum on INvestment Analysis
RETINA

This program calculates:
- Revenue Generated for the Academic Year
- Including Tuition and Formula Funding per Course
- Costs of Faculty Salaries
- ROI by Faculty, Departments, and Schools
- Expenditures on Research Assistants and Teaching Assistants
- Overhead Costs of a School or Department

If we wish to examine the data by program level, we need to separate costs by level of instruction. One issue that arises is how much salary should be assigned to particular courses when courses are the unit of analysis. This aspect of the calculation is important when comparing, for example, a graduate and undergraduate program. There are a number of considerations. One can apportion the salary on the basis of the number of students. However, there is an argument (often built into workload formulae) that graduate teaching is "more work" than undergraduate teaching and therefore should be assigned a disproportionate amount of resources. In contrast, there is an argument for equity; in essence, the salary a faculty member earns from teaching for one term should be divided equally among the courses that person teaches for that term. We have programmed RETINA using the latter argument. Figure 7.3 uses a diagram to show the RETINA methodology.

Another issue at our university is the relationship between the source of funding for the course and the home department of the instructor. While origin of funding is not a problem for many institutions, our university has a long history of interdisciplinary course work, and we have several professors (including one of the authors) who teach across departments and schools. For faculty who instruct in different areas, the funding derived from the formula and tuition flows to the academic unit paying the faculty. So, for example, if Professor Alpha holds tenure in the Department of Mathematics but teaches a course funded by Engineering, the Department of Engineering receives the benefits of formula and tuition generation. In short, the department that incurs the costs should also receive the revenue.

The following are variables taken into account when generating income from a class: level of the course (freshman to doctoral), type of course (lib-

Figure 7.3. Methodology for RETINA

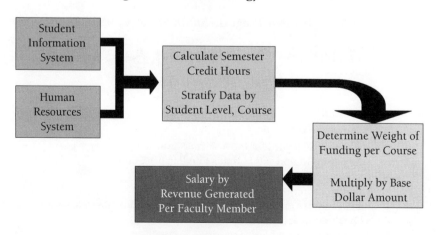

eral arts, engineering, science, and so on), level of student, and number of semester credit hours per course. Once these variables have been identified, they are processed through the formula funding weights to determine the value of the class and then multiplied by a set dollar amount by the state. As of 2007, tuition is controlled by guaranteed tuition plans that essentially fix student tuition and fees based on the year they enroll at the university. This new tuition plan required the construction of a separate program to capture the actual amount of tuition and fees collected per student in a course. The resultant file is then merged with the data produced from RETINA to produce the revenue generated per course. Figure 7.4 shows the formulas that are used to calculate formula funding revenue for the State of Texas higher education institutions.

Deans and program heads are tenured and therefore are included in the calculation of faculty costs. As noted above, faculty members who hold a position in a school but are not being paid by their school to teach were removed from that school's calculation. Both state salary funds and all salary funds were calculated for ROI calculations. Because this analysis focuses on teaching revenue and state funds, contracts and grants information is not included.

Results. Schools and departments obviously have faculty and staff who generate funds in addition to tuition, fees, and state appropriations, but this report is designed to guide administrators in their examination of funding source in relation to the activities that generate those funds. How

Figure 7.4. Formula Funding: Revenue Streams in Texas Public Higher Education

FORMULA FUNDING:
REVENUE STREAMS IN TEXAS PUBLIC
HIGHER EDUCATION

FORMULA VARIABLES

(F) - Funding
(M) - Multiplied Result
(D) - Dollar for Approval Funding Level
(L) - Lowest Common Denominator Funding
(W) - Weight Assigned to Course Type
(S) - Semester Credit Hours of the Course

$$(W)*(S) = (M)$$

$$(L)*(M)*(D) = (F)$$

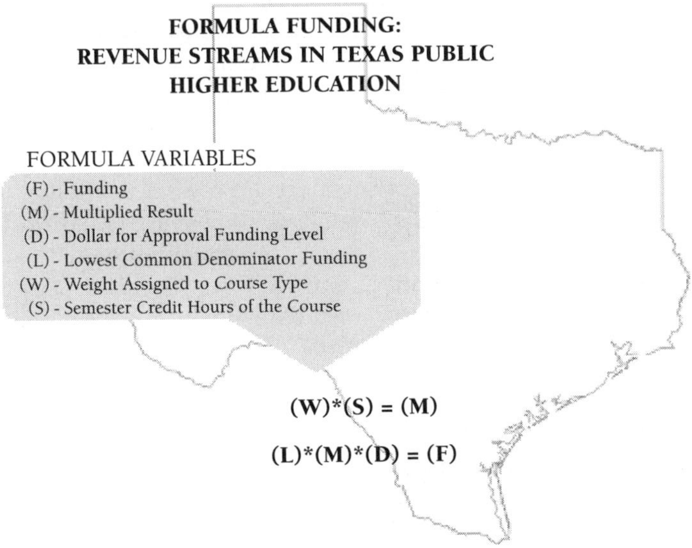

do we subsidize programs that are necessary but are not generating as much in state funds due to the classification of their programs by the state formula funding system? What personnel are needed to maximize ROI in different areas without sacrificing learning outcomes?

To begin the search for answers, we look at the schools and departments. An example of one type of RETINA output is provided. In Table 7.3, we have a hypothetical output for teaching faculty (including Teaching assistants with course responsibility). The figures show a great deal of variability, and there may (or may not) be sound administrative and policy reasons for this variability. The data frame the policy questions for the administrators (and for faculty). Figure 7.5 provides a histogram demonstrating the relationship of two professors in a hypothetical department of thirty-six faculty.

Arrayed in this manner, the data provide a clear policy issue and a point for discussion by the departmental chair in performance evaluations. Again there may be good reason for the distribution to appear as it does, but over time, one should expect changes in the ordering of faculty. As demonstrated in Figure 7.6, the accumulation of these data over time can tell a clear story about faculty who produce positive net revenue and those who do not (note that we are neither discussing teaching effectiveness nor learning outcomes). While we have admittedly considered two extreme examples, the figure demonstrates the power of RETINA for assisting with performance evaluations. In this example, both professors finished writing books in the fall of 2002 and were given course relief (as in small class sizes and reduced teaching loads) to finish their scholarly work. But observe what happens after fall semester of 2002. Clearly one professor is underperforming, while the other has a clear case for positive performance review.

The data in RETINA allow scalability in analysis. Because they build the database up from the course level (including individual instruction), the data can be arrayed in a variety of ways. Graduate programs can be compared to undergraduate programs, for example, and with other available data, administrative costs of these programs can be assigned and reviewed. Data can be examined for core versus noncore courses and for so-called gateway courses and their subsequent effects on courses that follow. Besides descriptive statistics, the RETINA database allows inferential work. Variables such as time of day, length of session, instructor evaluations, and drop rates can be combined in multivariate analyses. Demand elasticity for courses and instructors can be established, which can have an impact on creating more efficient course scheduling.

Concluding Observations

Resources are not infinite, and means of accountability allow close examination of the distribution of costs as part of an overall examination of the university. RETINA creates a comparative database to analyze productivity

Table 7.3. State of Texas Formula Funding Matrix

School	Department	Name	Percentage of Time on State Funds	Academic Year State Salary	Tuition and Formula Generated	Annual ROI for Tuition and Formula Funding—State Salary
LSA	FA	Adams, Don	50%	$2,000.00	$14,000.00	$12,000.00
ENG	CSE	Curtis, Tony	50%	$4,000.00	$14,000.00	$10,000.00
TA Subtotals				**$6,000.00**	**$28,000.00**	**$22,000.00**
LSA	HIST	Bacon, Kevin	100%	$2,250.00	$13,000.00	$10,750.00
ENG	CSE	Scott, Mon.	100%	$3,250.00	$6,000.00	$2,750.00
ENG	ME	Larson, Gary	100%	$21,250.00	$37,000.00	$15,750.00
SCE	BIO	Rembrant, C.	100%	$4,250.00	$55,000.00	$50,750.00
Lecturers Subtotal				**$31,000.0**	**$111,000.00**	**$80,000.00**
LSA	SOC	Brown, Charlie	100%	$40,000.00	$180,000.00	$140,000.00
ENG	CSE	King, Stephan	100%	$75,000.00	$71,000.00	($4,000.00)
ENG	SOF	Kirk, James T.	100%	$40,000.00	$89,000.00	$49,000.00
SCE	AST	Simpson, Lisa	100%	$60,000.00	$89,000.00	$29,000.00
Tenure-Track Faculty Subtotal				**$215,000.00**	**$429,000.00**	**$214,000.00**
LSA	LIT	Adams, Scott	100%	$55,000.00	$85,000.00	$30,000.00
ENG	SOF	Gates, Bill	90%	$120,000.00	$31,000.00	($89,000.00)
ENG	SOF	Jobs, Steve	88%	$175,000.00	$230,000.00	$55,000.00
SCE	PSY	Hartley, Robert	100%	$70,000.00	$114,000.00	$44,000.00
SCE	BIO	Cousteau, J.	90%	$38,000.00	$0.00	($38,000.00)
SCE	BIO	Irwin, Steve	89%	$76,000.00	$335,000.00	$259,000.00
SCE	BIO	Irwin, Terri	89%	$76,000.00	$270,000.00	$194,000.00
SCE	PHY	Bond, James	89%	$80,000.00	$25,000.00	($55,000.00)
Tenured Faculty Subtotal				**$690,000.00**	**$1,090,000.00**	**$400,000.00**
Grand Total for the University				**$942,000.00**	**$1,658,000.00**	**$716,000.00**

Figure 7.5. Histogram of Revenue Outliers

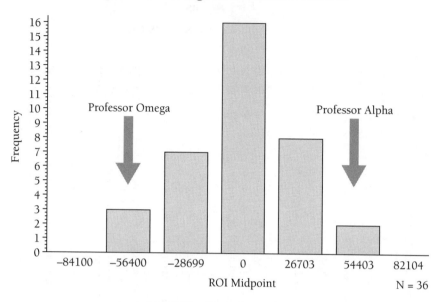

Annual ROI($) — Formula Funding — State Funds

Source: UTD Office of Strategic Planning and Analysis.

in terms of resource inputs and revenue generation and provides insights into rationales for making resource allocations. RETINA, as part of the larger database, allows examination of the drivers of performance (course, instructor, time of offering) and relative overhead costs by academic unit, thus promoting efficiencies and accountability. With student flow data, RETINA allows an analysis of the dependency relationships between academic units. As such, RETINA is a robust decision analysis tool. It can help administrators differentiate between departments that struggle financially, but are necessary to the overall academic curriculum of the school, and departments that are wasteful, inefficient, or support programs that are esoteric or not viable as seen in Exhibit 7.1.

Detailed analyses of overhead costs and revenue generation have an important place in higher education. Such information guides colleges and universities as they seek to control costs, streamline operations, and improve the quality and effectiveness of the educational experiences of their students. Resources can be redirected to bolster efficient yet struggling departments, industrious faculty can be identified and rewarded, and underperforming faculty can be counseled to improve their performance.

NEW DIRECTIONS FOR INSTITUTIONAL RESEARCH • DOI: 10.1002/ir

Figure 7.6. Examining Return on Investment in Performance Evaluations

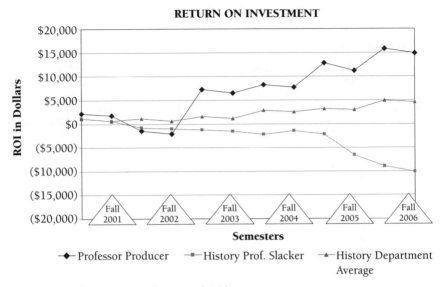

RETURN ON INVESTMENT

Source: UTD Office of Strategic Planning and Analysis.

Although RETINA cannot track faculty with administrative duties or research, it can be used in tandem with other measures and data (such as contract and grant information and teaching evaluations) to yield a clearer picture of the effectiveness of a program or department. RETINA is not a

Exhibit 7.1. Summary of Concluding Observations

RETINA allows for a comparative database to analyze productivity and provides traditional means of making resource allocations.

RETINA promotes efficiencies and accountability.

RETINA as part of the larger database allows for examination of the drivers of performance (course, instructor, time of offering, etc.) and relative overhead costs by academic unit.

RETINA allows for "what if" revenue/costs projection scenarios under various growth, status quo and enrollment declines.

With Student Flow data, RETINA allows for an analysis of the dependency relationships between academic units. As such it is a robust decision analysis tool.

panacea but rather a tool designed to enable colleges and universities to provide the finest educational services possible to their communities while simultaneously using their resources with great economy and wisdom.

References

Purcell, Jr., W. *Understanding a Company's Finances.* New York: Barnes and Noble, 1983.
Redlinger, L., and Gordon, S. "Determining what It Costs to Teach a College Course." Presentation at the 2005 AIR Forum, San Diego, Calif., June 2005.
Texas Higher Education Coordinating Board. *Formula Funding Information from the Texas Higher Education Coordinating Board.* 2008. Retrieved Sept. 9, 2008, from http://www.thecb.state.tx.us/Reports/PDF/1192.PDF.
Winston, G. "Why Can't a College Be More Like a Firm?" *Change,* 1997, 29(5), 33–38.

LAWRENCE J. REDLINGER *is a professor and the executive director for the office of strategic planning and analysis at the University of Texas at Dallas.*

NICOLAS A. VALCIK *is the associate director for the office of strategic planning and analysis and an assistant clinical professor for the Program of Public Affairs at the University of Texas at Dallas.*

8

This concluding chapter focuses on issues of the current economic market that are affecting college and university sources of revenue, as well their ability to hire and retain quality faculty.

The Role Institutional Research Plays in Navigating the Current Economic Uncertainty

Mary Beth Worley

Nationally, state spending for public higher education has been declining as a proportion of state general fund expenditures. Traditionally state-appropriated budgets for public colleges and universities tend to be cut during times of economic crisis, but often these funds are not always restored once the crisis has passed. As a result "the average percentage of state general fund expenditures devoted to public higher education declined by 37 percent nationally from 1974 to 2001" (Tandberg, 2008, p. 3). This chapter discusses the recent downturn in the U.S. economy and how this decline affects college and university budgets, student financial aid, and the need for an institution to have an institutional research office that can provide timely and meaningful data to address these recent events.

Legislative Funding

In May 2008, the president of the University of Florida announced a plan to cut $47 million from the university's 2008–2009 budget in response to the $512 million statewide budget cuts approved by the Florida State Legislature. As a result of these cuts, the university stated that it would "reduce funding for administrative units, research, reduce or eliminate degrees and courses, and restructure several departments" ("UF Reduces Spending by

NEW DIRECTIONS FOR INSTITUTIONAL RESEARCH, no. 140, Winter 2008 © Wiley Periodicals, Inc.
Published online in Wiley InterScience (www.interscience.wiley.com) • DOI: 10.1002/ir.273

$47 Million," 2008, p. 1). Approximately 430 positions will be eliminated, of which 20 non-tenured faculty and 118 staff are expected to be laid off. Undergraduate enrollment will be reduced by four thousand students over a four-year period, with the first year affecting about one thousand transfer students.

Another example of financial stress at the state level that will affect higher education can be found in California. Governor Arnold Schwarzenegger announced that the three California higher education systems may, along with most other state agencies, lose 10 percent of their proposed annual budgets, or nearly $1.3 billion between them, under the governor's spending plan for the fiscal year that begins July 1, 2008 (Leff, 2008).

The greatest portion of a university's or college's operating expenditure budget is usually earmarked for faculty salaries and benefits. With the recent downturn in the U.S. economy, examining faculty pay may be a more important part in the budget review process than in the recent past. Chapters Five and Seven offer two models that administrators can use for strategic planning and performance-based decision making. As budgets continue to be cut in public institutions of higher education, administrators will be required to assess how resources are being distributed and determine if those resources are being used in the best interest of the students and the goals of the institution.

Economic Market and Retaining Faculty

In 2007, the University of Wisconsin System released a report stating that after adjusting for inflation, state appropriations to the university system have declined since 2000 while enrollment at institutions has increased. Although revenues from other sources have increased over time, these revenues are often restricted to uses other than instruction. The conclusion of the study is that the decrease in state-appropriated funds will make it difficult for the university system to "maintain funding for student instruction" (Clark, 2007). In April 2008, the *Chronicle of Higher Education* reported that "Wisconsin's stagnating state higher-education budget has forced the university to keep faculty salaries far below average. When professors get feelers from elsewhere, they learn that a move can easily mean a whopping 100-percent salary increase—sometimes more" (Wilson, 2008).

The California Postsecondary Education Commission reported that compensation for faculty at California's public universities has failed to keep pace with peer institutions and that the "decline in quality will have a ripple effect throughout the state, one from which it may take decades to recover" (Academic Senate of the CSU, 2005).

In Chapter Four, Herzog proposes a four-step approach for analyzing faculty compensation equity for instructional faculty at a public land grant university. This model allows the inclusion of performance-based internal factors as well as external factors such as market forces, including national salary comparators measures of career progression.

Merit-Based Scholarships and Private Loans

In April 2008 the Kentucky Higher Education Student Loan Corporation, also known as the Student Loan People, announced that the agency will suspend making college loans to first-time borrowers beginning in May 2008, affecting some twenty-seven thousand Kentucky college students (Jester, 2008). The agency cited fallout from the national market crisis as the reason for the decision to suspend first-time student loans.

By May 5, 2008, *Forbes* magazine (Zumbrun, 2008) reported that the Federal Reserve took action that will allow student loan lenders who were unable to sell packages of student loans in the secondary markets the opportunity to "swap them for safe Treasury bills." The article also reported that the U.S. House and Senate passed a bill temporarily authorizing the Department of Education to be able to purchase government-backed loans and extend the size of federally guaranteed loans that lenders can offer. President Bush signed the bill into legislation on May 7, 2008.

Many states rely on state-supported financial aid programs to help improve access to higher education. Chapter Six contains a discussion of one such program: the Kentucky lottery (KEES) merit-based scholarship program. Since 1999, the total value earned by Kentucky's merit-based scholarship program has more than tripled, from $13 million to more than $44 million in 2007, and by 2010 the amount is projected to be more than $47 million. Also, the number of students receiving at least one base award increased from 29,835 students in 1999 to 37,741 in 2007. The number of recipients in 2010 is projected to be almost 40,000.

Because the KEES program is funded by revenues from the state lottery sales, it is possible that these sales will not be able to meet the needs of all eligible students. According to the 2007 Kentucky Lottery Annual Report, ticket sales for 2007 were at an all-time high, resulting in operating revenues of $744.2 million compared to $742.3 million in 2006. However, due to an increase in prize payouts, the gross profits decreased 4.5 percent, from $232 million in 2007 compared to $242.9 million in 2006. This resulted in a decrease of approximately $1.7 million in payments made to the KEES scholarship reserve fund for 2007 (Commonwealth of Kentucky, 2007). McCrary and Condrey (2003) suggest "that lottery-generated funds may reach a plateau or peak during the first decade of implementation and that state policymakers should design lottery-funded programs accordingly" (p. 691). In fact, states including New Hampshire, Arizona, Florida, and Tennessee have reported a decline in lottery sales for the first quarter of the 2008 fiscal year.

The forecasting model the KHEAA uses relies on historic KEES data to forecast the number of graduates who will earn the award and the average award amount used toward each postsecondary year of education. Although the forecasting model may be accurate in predicting the funds needed for all eligible recipients, it is essential that KHEAA monitor the profits of the lottery in order to be prepared to respond to a decrease in payments to the KEES fund.

New Directions for Institutional Research • DOI: 10.1002/ir

The Importance of Accurate and Meaningful Data

With the availability of powerful and inexpensive personal computers as well as enterprise-level database systems, institutional researchers have an improved ability to access various institutional data. However, some colleges and universities that are using these more powerful technologies have been slow to move away from the "autocratic and centralized control of access to low level data" mind-set of the previous generation of mainframe technology. Levy suggests in Chapter Three that "many of the hopes and promises regarding the ease of reporting and access to data that were proffered as enterprise systems spread have never borne fruit" possibly due to the organizational politics and out-of-date technology policies and practices.

In overcoming the obstacle of the institution's self-imposed barriers that prevent or limit the institutional researcher's access to important information such as human resource faculty data and cost data, the college or university must first adopt a commitment to the concept of institutional data and data custodians, trustee, and stewards rather than data owners of specific departmental or unit data. Institutions that have embraced the concept of institutional data and adjusted their data access policies accordingly recognize the value of institutional data as a resource and improve accuracy of the data through its widespread use. In Chapter Two, Valcik and Stigdon suggest that the ability of the institutional researcher to effectively work with the many subcultures within a university or college allows the opportunity for participants in the administrative process to "integrate their knowledge toward organizational assessment and obtain important feedback" regarding the administrative process.

Conclusion

In this volume, the focus is on challenges that institutional research offices face when analyzing financial and human resource data in providing timely, accurate, and meaningful data for federal- and state-mandated reports, as well as for internal strategic planning and policymaking. Providing this meaningful and accurate information is possible only when the institutional research office is provided access to the necessary databases from which to gather the data.

Nearly forty years ago, Bolman (1970) wrote that "institutional research must begin today to take a far broader and more penetrating look at our institutions of higher education, and our administrators and faculty must act quickly on the basis of sound planning and not just wait for each crisis to erupt" (p. 88). This statement still holds true today. With the existing financial market crisis, it is imperative that institutional research offices be able to respond quickly—for example, by providing important information to administrators regarding the effects of a decrease in state-appropriated budgets funds, determining if the institution is offering competitive faculty compensation to retain quality faculty, and projecting changes in the availability of financial aid or merit-based scholarships or other key sources of revenue. Financial and human resource data clearly can help inform and improve the strategic planning initiatives at colleges and universities, and offices of institutional research should be at the forefront in helping their institutions use this information.

References

Academic Senate of the CSU. "Faculty Compensation and the Crisis in Recruiting and Retaining Faculty of High Quality." May 2005. Retrieved May 11, 2008, from http://www.calstate.edu/AcadSen/Records/Reports/statement_on_faculty_salariesfinal.pdf.

Bolman, F. "University Reform and Institutional Research." *Journal of Higher Education,* 1970, *41*(2), 85–97.

Clark, K. "Declines in Spending on Public Higher Education in Wisconsin: An Analysis of the University of Wisconsin System Budget." Wisconsin Center for the Advancement of Postsecondary Education. Madison: University of Wisconsin–Madison, 2007. Retrieved May 7, 2008, from http://www.wiscape.wisc.edu/publications/wb003/documents/WB003.pdf.

Commonwealth of Kentucky. "Report of the Audit of the Kentucky Lottery Corporation for the Years Ended June 30, 2007 and 2006." Commonwealth of Kentucky, Auditor of Public Accounts, 2007. Retrieved May 11, 2008, from http://www.kylottery.com/apps/export/system/modules/com.kyl.site/galleries/documents/KYLottery_annual_report/2007x2006KYLotteryaudit.pdf.

"UF Reduces Spending by $47 Million in Response to State Budget Reductions." *Inside UF,* May 5, 2008. Retrieved May 7, 2008, from http://insideuf.ufl.edu/2008/05/05/budget-cuts-2/.

Jester, A. "Loans for 27,000 Students in Doubt: State Agency Says Credit Crisis Has Cut into Funds." *kentucky.com,* Apr. 19, 2008. Retrieved May 7, 2008, from http://www.tradingmarkets.com/.site/news/Stock%20News/1397185/.

Leff, L. "California Higher Ed Leaders Denounce Proposed Budget Cuts." *signonsandiego.com,* Apr. 28, 2008. Retrieved May 11, 2008, from http://www.signonsandiego.com/news/state/20080428-1625-ca-collegecosts.html.

McCrary, J., and Condrey, S. "The Georgia Lottery: Assessing Its Administrative, Economic, and Political Effects." *Review of Policy Research,* 2003, *20*(4), 691–711.

Tandberg, D. "The Politics of State Higher Education Funding." *Higher Education in Review,* 2008, *5,* 1–36.

Wilson, R. "Wisconsin's Flagship Is Raided for Scholars: Public Institutions Can't Match Job Offers from Private Universities." *Chronicle.com,* Apr. 18, 2008. Retrieved May 7, 2008, from http://chronicle.com/weekly/v54/i32/32a00103.htm.

Zumbrun, J. "Student Loans Shine Again." *Forbes.com,* May 5, 2008. Retrieved May 7, 2008, from http://www.forbes.com/business/2008/05/05/fed-sallie-loans-biz-beltway-cx_jz_0505studentloans.html.

MARY BETH WORLEY is the coordinator of institutional research for the office of institutional effectiveness and planning at New Mexico State University—Doña Ana Community College.

INDEX

Academic faculty data, 53–54
Academic Senate of the CSU, 110
Academic year SCHs, 66
Account types, and personnel information, 22–23
Administrative process: and organizational theory, 15–16; and support staff, 16
Aiken, L., 58
Allen, R., 26
American Association of University Professors, 15
Argent Global Services, 1
Armstrong, K., 28, 37
Arreola, R., 29
Ashraf, J., 51
Association of American Medical Colleges, 60
Association to Advance Collegiate Schools of Business (AACSB), 54, 60

Balzer, W., 50
Banner, 32
Barbezat, D., 50
Barr, M., 25
Becker, W., 51
Bellas, M., 51
Berlin Wall, fall of, 5
Binary logistic regression, 52
Birnbaum, R., 40
Bolman, F., 112
Boudreau, N., 51
Bowen, H., 25
Braden, I., 49
Braskamp, L., 49
Brinkman, P., 26, 27
Brown, W., 37
Business and human resources data: analyzing/using, 5–11; navigating economic uncertainty using, 10

Canavos, G., 50
Canonical correlation, 8, 52–53
Carlin, P., 50
Carnevale, D., 5
Carrigan, S., 9, 65, 78

Civil Rights Act (1964), Title VII of, 49
Clark, K., 110
Classification of Instructional Programs (CIP) discipline, 66
COBOL, 19
Cohen, J., 58
Cohen, P., 58
Collaborative software, 6
College and University Personnel Association, 14
College and University Professional Association, 60
Commission on Higher Education, 6
Commonwealth of Kentucky, 111
Condrey, S., 111

Dalton, M., 60
Data integrity, 7
Data trustees, 33–34
Datatel, 32
Decision makers, 6
Delaware Study, 9, 66–67; academic program benchmarks, 67; enrollment targets report, 72–74; normative data perspectives, 72; trend report, 75–76
Departmental scorecard, 40
Dino, G., 60
Distance education, 5–6
Dual appointments, and reporting, 21–22
Duncan, K., 50
Dyke, F., 26

Ehrenberg, R., 50
Enterprise-level relational database systems, 32
Equal Pay Act (1963), 49

Facilities data, analysis of, 7
Faculty compensation model, 49–64; academic faculty data, 53–54; age, and rank/tenure, 55; analytical approach, 52–53; binary logistic regression, 52; canonical correlation, 52–53; canonical correlation analysis, 55–57; canonical functions, dimension reduction

115

data for (table), 55; fields of study/ degrees, by gender, 55; methodological issues, 49–51; misclassified tenure-status cases, hypothetical characteristics of, 57; multinomial logistic regression, 52–53; multiple linear regression, 52; nonmedical school faculty, salary prediction of, 58–59; omitted variable bias, 50, 52; performance, 54; salary adjustment criteria, development of, 60–61; salary adjustment, determining, 58–61; salary analyses, variables used in (table), 53–54; salary regression models, 50; selection bias, 51; selection screens, developing, 61; systematic bias, measuring, 54–58; tenure/tenure-track status, 52–53; underpaid individuals, 61

Faculty composition, 6

Faculty salary equity analysis, approach for performing, 8–9

Faculty scorecard, 40–41

Family Educational Rights and Privacy Act (FERPA), 18–19

Federal Privacy Act (1974), 18

Ferber, M., 49

Fidell, L., 52

Financial Accounting Standards Board, 26

Financial stress, affecting higher education, 110

Fish, L., 51

FOCUS (programming language), 19

Foster, A., 5

Friedman, T., 5

Fuhs, F., 50

Funding formulas and guidelines, 65

Gaber, C., 37

Gater, D., 30, 31

Gaylord, C., 60

Gordon, N., 49

Gordon, S., 95

Gortner, H., 2

Governmental Accounting Standards Board, 26

Graham, R., 37

Graves, P., 50

Haignere, L., 50, 51

Hample, S., 25

Hellriegel, D., 1

Henson, R., 55

Herzog, S., 8–9, 50, 64

Higher Education Reorganization Act (1971), 65

Hignite, K., 6

HRS DB2, 19

Hughes, J., 50

Human resource and finance data, analysis of, 7

Human resource information system, 23

Human resources faculty data/cost data: accessing, 31–34; beginner's guide, 25–47; data-access policies, 32, 34; data stewards, 33–34; data trustees, 33–34; expenditure/cost functions, 27–28; expenditure/cost objects, 26–27; higher education cost data concepts, 26–29; higher education human resource faculty data concepts, types of, 29–31; integrating, 34–44; ratios to facilitate decision making, 39; student data, ownership of, 33; University of Delaware Study of Instructional Costs and Productivity, 35–37, 44

Hurst, P., 26

Hyer, P., 60

Incremental (baseline) budgeting, 65

Institutional data, 10

Institutional research, 7–8, 10–11, 13, 23; accurate and meaningful data, 112; economic market and retaining faculty, 110; and federal confidentiality laws, 19; and institutional data, 32; and integrated knowledge, 16, 25; legislative funding, 109–110; merit-based scholarships, 111; private loans, 111; role in navigating current economic uncertainty, 109–113; salary data, 15

Integrated human resources faculty data/ cost data, 34–44; scorecard notion, 40–41

Integrated Postsecondary Education Data System (IPEDS), 8, 26; faculty, definition of, 30; Fall Staff Survey, 29–31; Fringe Benefits of Full-Time Instructional Faculty Survey, 29–30; full-time instructional faculty, definition of, 30; Human Resources surveys, 29, 39, 44; instruction, definition of, 30; Salary survey, 31; staff and faculty reports, 22; surveys, 13–14, 29–30

Isaacs, H., 37

Jamison, C., 1
Jester, A., 111
Johnson, D., 49

Kaplan, R., 40
Kentucky Council on Postsecondary Education, 82, 85
Kentucky Educational Excellence Scholarship (KEES) program, 84–86, 111; average award amounts, 90; awards, 82; budget process, 84–86; budget projections, 86; budgeting for, 79–92; Consensus Forecast Group, 91; data, 84; defined, 80; disbursement data, 84; earned awards by high school graduating cohort (table), 89; earnings rates, 89; eligibility, 81–82; eligibility data, 84; forecasting award amounts, 89–91; forecasting use of, 86–88; KEES Consensus Forecast Group (KCFG), 85; projected disbursements, 87–88; and state lottery sales, 111; utilization, 83
Kentucky Educational Excellence Scholarship program, 9
Kentucky General Assembly: and KEES budget, 84; Senate Bill 21, 79–80
Kentucky Higher Education Assistance Authority (KHEAA), 9, 80–81, 91; base and bonus award schedule, 81; defined, 84; GoHigher Web site, 80; and KEES budget, 85
Kentucky Higher Education Student Loan Corporation, 111
Kentucky Revised Statutes, 79
Krall, L., 50

Layzell, D., 65
Lean Enterprise Process, 1
Leff, L., 110
Letteer, M., 9, 79
Levy, G.D., 7–8, 25, 47
Loeb, J., 49, 50
Logistic regression, 8–9
Lombardi, J., 30, 31
Luna, A., 50

Mahler, J., 2
Marchand, J., 50
Markov chain, 71
Matier, R., 26
Maxey, J., 50
McCrary, J., 111
McGraw, M., 50

McLaughlin, G., 49, 60
Middaugh, M., 25, 35–37, 38
Milam, J., 26
Minter, J., 37
Montgomery, J., 49
Moore, J., 51
Moore, N., 50, 52, 61, 62
Morton, T., 49
Mrdjenovic, J., 50
Multinomial logistic regression, 8–9, 52–53
Multiple linear regression, 52

National Association of College and University Business Officers, 26
National Center for Education Statistics (NCES), 13; Web site, 31
National Science Foundation reports, 22
National Study of Instructional Costs and Productivity, See Delaware Study
Nelson, M., 31
Neumark, D., 50
Nicholson, J., 2
North Carolina Community College System funding formulas, 65
Norton, D., 40

Oaxaca, R., 50
Oklahoma State University Salary study, 45, 54
Omitted variable bias, 50, 52
Oracle, 32
Organizational assessment, 16
Organizational theory, and administrative process, 15–16
Outdated policies, and institutional data, 10

Patton, Paul, 79
Payroll system, and personnel information, 23
PeopleSoft, 32
Performance contracting, 65
Personnel and financial data: budget file vs. payroll data, 21–23; computer resources, 19–21; Family Educational Rights and Privacy Act (FERPA), 18–19; mining, key issues with, 16–23; reports that use, 13–15; subcultures within a university, working with, 15–16; University of Texas at Dallas (UT-Dallas) computer resources, 19–21; using for reporting purposes, 13–24

Personnel information, and account types, 22–23

Pfeffer, J., 1

Prus, M., 50

Public accountability of colleges/universities, 6

Purcell, W. Jr., 96

Rapidly changing work environment, 6–7

Recruitment, of faculty/staff, 6

Redlinger, L.J., 2, 10, 93, 95, 108

RETINA (RETurn on INvestment Analysis) program, 95, 99–104, 106–107; defined, 99; faculty salary information, use of, 100; formula funding, 103, 105; information sources, 101; limitations, 100–102; methodology, 100–103; modification of (2007), 99; objectives of, 99; output, 104; and performance evaluations, 104, 107; results, 103–104; revenue outliers, histogram of, 104, 106; as robust decision analysis tool, 106–108; scalability in analysis, 104; summary of calculations, 101

Return on investment (ROI) analysis, 10

Return on investment (ROI) models, 93–108; defined, 94; design of, 95; infrastructure support formula, 95–97; instruction and operations formula, 95; RETINA (RETurn on INvestment Analysis) program, 95, 99–104, 106–107; special assignments, 98–99; state formula funding, 97–98; and students as revenue generators, 94–95

Rooney, P., 50

Salary analyses, variables used in (table), 53–54

Sanders, L., 26, 32

Schwarzeneger, Arnold, 110

Scorecard notion, 40–41; sample faculty scorecard, psychology department, 42–43; sample psychology departmental scorecard, 40–41

Scott, E., 49

Scott, R., 15, 16

Selection bias, 51

Semester credit hours (SCHs), 66

Sexton, R., 50

Shahid, A., 37

Sherry, A., 55

Sidle, C., 26

Simpson, W., 26

Slocum, J. Jr., 1

Smart, J., 49

Snyder, J., 60

Social Security Act (1990), 18

Southern Association of Colleges and Schools (SACS), 6, 13

Spelling, M., 6

Spinelli, M., 50

Standard error of estimate (SEE), 58

Stevens, J., 52

Stewart, K., 60

Stigdon, A.D., 7, 13, 24, 32, 112

Strathman, J., 50, 51

Student and Exchange Visitor Information System tracking, 15

Subcultures: questions enabling interaction of, 17; relationship of university data to, 17; working with, 15–16

Sun, M., 60

Supplemental pay for faculty, reporting of, 23

Support staff, and administrative process, 16

Sybase, 32

Tabachnick, B., 52

Tandberg, D., 109

Technological advances, and information sharing, 5

Technology-delivered education, 5–6

Texas Higher Education Coordinating Board, 14, 18, 22, 96, 97

Title VII, Civil Rights Act (1964), 49

Toutkoushian, R., 50, 51, 61

Unequal pay, 49–50

University of Delaware, Study of Instructional Costs and Productivity, 35–37, 44

University of North Carolina at Greensboro (UNCG), 67, 71–72, 77; classroom productivity and comparable Delaware Study norms, collection of, 72

University of North Carolina (UNC) system, 65–66; credit hour production report, 67; department review, 74–77; enrollment change funding at campus level, 71–72; enrollment change model, 71; enrollment targets, setting, 72–74; funding formulas, 65; funding matrix, 68–71; funding model, 65–66; SCH projections at campus level, 71–72

University of Texas at Dallas (UT-Dallas): computer resources, 19–21; Office of Strategic Planning and Analysis, 23
University of Wisconsin system, decline in state appropriations to, 110
U.S. Department of Education, 6, 13

Valcik, N.A., 4, 7, 10, 13, 24, 32, 93, 108, 112
Volkwein, J., 26
Voucher system, 65

Wallace, R.H., 5, 11
Watt, C., 7
Weistroffer, H., 50
West, S., 58
Wilkinson, S., 60
Wilson, R., 110
Winston, G.C., 26, 94
World Is Flat, The: A Brief History of the Twenty-First Century (Friedman), 5
Worley, M.B., 10, 109, 113

Zumbrun, J., 111

OTHER TITLES AVAILABLE IN THE
NEW DIRECTIONS FOR INSTITUTIONAL RESEARCH SERIES
Robert K. Toutkoushian, Editor-in-Chief

IR139   Conducting Institutional Research in Non-Campus-Based Settings
Robert K. Toutkoushian, Tod R. Massa
One aspect of the institutional research (IR) profession that has not been
well documented is the many ways that this research is carried out beyond
the confines of a traditional campus-based IR office. The purpose of this
volume of *New Directions for Institutional Research* is to provide readers with
insight into some of these alternatives and help expand understanding of the
nature of institutional research. The chapters in this volume show how
institutional research is being conducted by public university system offices,
state higher education coordinating boards, institutional-affiliated research
offices, and higher education consultants. Because these entities often do not
have ready access to campus-specific data, they must be creative in finding
ways to obtain data and information that enable them to provide a value-
added function in the field. The chapter authors highlight ways in which
these offices acquire and use information for institutional research.
ISBN: 978-04704-12749

IR138   Legal Applications of Data for Institutional Research
Andrew L. Luna
This volume of *New Directions for Institutional Research* explores the seem-
ingly incongruent forces of statistical reasoning and the law and sheds some
light on how institutional researchers can use the two in a complementary
manner to prevent a legal action or to help support the rebuttal of a prima
facie case (i.e., one that at first glance presents sufficient evidence for the
plaintiff to win the case). Until now, there has been little linkage between
the disciplines of law and statistics. While the legal profession uses statistics
to support an argument, interpretations of statistical outcomes may not
follow scientific reasoning. Similarly, a great piece of statistical theory or a
tried-and-true methodology among institutional research professionals may
be thrown out of court if it fails to meet the rules of evidence or contradicts
current legal standing. The information contained within this volume will
benefit institutional research practitioners and contribute to a more frequent
dialogue concerning the complexities of statistical science within the legal
environment.
ISBN: 978-04703-97619

IR137   Alternative Perspectives in Institutional Planning
Terry T. Ishitani
Institutional planning is coming to the fore in higher education as states,
the federal government, and the public increasingly demand accountability.
Institutional researchers, the data stewards for colleges and universities,
are becoming involved in such strategic planning, supporting efforts to
strengthen institutional efficiency and effectiveness in policymaking.
Researchers find that locating, preparing, and presenting necessary data
and information for planners is a challenging exercise. In this volume of *New
Directions for Institutional Research*, administrators, consultants, researchers,
and scholars provide unique, innovative approaches to that challenge. Some
authors introduce program applications and statistical techniques; others
share case studies. The variety of perspectives and depths of focus makes
this a timely, useful guide for institutional researchers.
ISBN: 978-04703-84534

IR136   Using Qualitative Methods in Institutional Assessment
Shaun R. Harper, Samuel D. Museus
This volume of *New Directions for Institutional Research* advocates the broad
use of qualitative methods in assessment across American higher education:
campus cultures, academic success and retention programs, student
experiences and learning, and teaching effectiveness. The chapter authors
suggest that responses to demands for increased accountability will be
insufficient if researchers continue to rely almost exclusively on statistical
analyses to assess institutional effectiveness. Instead, they recommend a
variety of qualitative approaches that can produce rich and instructive data
to guide institutional decision-making and action. In addition, they dispel
common myths and misconceptions regarding the use of qualitative methods
in assessment.
ISBN: 978-04702-83615

IR135   Space: The Final Frontier for Institutional Research
Nicholas A. Valcik
Facilities information, once a world of precious drawings and laborious
calculations, has been transformed by the power of information technology.
Blueprints securely locked in cabinets have given way to online systems
based on geospatial information systems (GIS). The result is nimble systems
adaptable to purposes across administrations, applications that integrate
divisions—business, institutional research, student affairs—with shared
information. This volume of *New Directions for Institutional Research* delves
into this new world of facilities information. The authors show how to
gather data and how state and other agencies use it. They discuss the
necessity of accurate, accessible information for determining and apportion-
ing indirect costs. They look at its use for student recruitment and retention, and they demonstrate how it can even be used to correlate various
classroom attributes with student learning success. With twenty-first-
century technology, facilities data is useful far beyond traditional business
affairs operations—it has become integral to institutional planning and
operation.
ISBN: 978-04702-55254

IR134   Advancing Sustainability in Higher Education
Larry H. Litten, Dawn Geronimo Terkla
Effective organizations strive constantly to improve. Colleges and universities
are becoming increasingly aware of financial, social, and environmental
challenges—both to their continued well-being and to the societies they
serve—many of which are subsumed under the category of sustainability.
In order to maintain progress, manage risk, and conserve resources,
policymakers and managers need information that monitors performance,
illuminates risk, and demonstrates responsible institutional behavior.
Institutional researchers bring distinctive knowledge and skills to the table.
This volume of *New Directions for Institutional Research* identifies various
obstacles to sustainable progress and describes solutions for advancing
educational institutions and the societies in which they are embedded.
ISBN: 978-04701-76870

IR133   Using Quantitative Data to Answer Critical Questions
Frances K. Stage
This volume of *New Directions for Institutional Research* challenges
quantitative researchers to become more critical. By providing examples
from the work of several prominent researchers, and by offering concrete
recommendations, the editor and authors deliver messages that are likely to
cause many educational researchers to reexamine their own work. The
collective efforts described here will help readers become more sensitive to

the nuances among various educational groups, and to pay more attention to outliers. This volume supplies both motivation and analytical support to those who might incorporate criticality into their own quantitative work, as well as to those who wish to read critical perspectives with an open mind about what they might find.
ISBN: 978-07879-97786

IR132   **Applying Economics to Institutional Research**
Robert K. Toutkoushian, Michael B. Paulsen
In many ways, economic concepts, models, and methods can be applied to higher education research. This volume's chapter authors are all higher education researchers with graduate training in economics and extensive experience in institutional research. They share insight on the economist's perspective of education costs and revenues, plus how to use economics to inform enrollment management and to understand faculty labor market issues.
ISBN: 978-07879-95768

IR131   **Data Mining in Action: Case Studies of Enrollment Management**
Jing Luan, Chun-Mei Zhao
Data mining has great potential to enhance institutional research. Six case studies in this volume employed data mining for solving real-world problems in enrollment yield, retention, transfer-outs, utilization of advanced-placement scores, predicting graduation rates, and more. Discusses data mining vs. traditional statistics, debunks the myths, and highlights the need for individual pattern recognition and customized treatment of students.
ISBN: 0-7879-9426-X

IR130   **Reframing Persistence Research to Improve Academic Success**
Edward P. St. John, Michael Wilkerson
This volume proposes and tests new collaborations between institutional researchers and others on campus who are engaged in breaking down barriers to academic success, especially for minorities and nontraditional students. What if traditional recommendations aren't effective? Chapters review prior research and best practices, then investigate new approaches to assessment, action research, action inquiry, and evaluation. Lessons learned can inform strategies of administrators, faculty, and everyone interested in improving success for all students.
ISBN: 0-7879-8759-X

IR129   **Analyzing Faculty Work and Rewards: Using Boyer's Four Domains of Scholarship**
John M. Braxton
Boyer's four domains—scholarships of discovery, application, integration, and teaching—influence and define scholars as their professional roles, career stages, and research goals change. This volume offers practical suggestions for academic reward structure, graduate school preparation, and state policy.
ISBN: 0-7879-8674-7

IR128   **Workforce Development and Higher Education: A Strategic Role for Institutional Research**
Richard A. Voorhees, Lee Harvey
Workforce development is a growing area for higher education. This volume examines its conceptual underpinnings from an international perspective, and it provides practical institutional case studies and specific techniques for gauging the market potential for new instructional programs. It discusses suggested projects and studies for IR personnel to consider on their campuses.
ISBN: 0-7879-8365-9

IR127 **Survey Research: Emerging Issues**
Paul D. Umbach
Demands for accountability are forcing colleges and universities to conduct
more high-quality surveys to gauge institutional effectiveness. New
technologies are improving survey implementation as well as researchers'
ability to effectively analyze data. This volume examines these emerging
issues in a rapidly changing environment and highlights lessons learned
from past research.
ISBN: 0-7879-8329-2

IR126 **Enhancing Alumni Research: European and American Perspectives**
David J. Weerts, Javier Vidal
The increasing globalization of higher education has made it easy to
compare problems, goals, and tools associated with conducting alumni
research worldwide. This research is also being used to learn about the
impact, purposes, and successes of higher education. This volume will help
institutional leaders use alumni research to respond to the increasing
demands of state officials, accrediting agencies, employers, prospective
students, parents, and the general public.
ISBN: 0-7879-8228-8

IR125 **Minority Retention: What Works?**
Gerald H. Gaither
Examines some of the best policies, practices, and procedures to achieve
greater diversity and access, while controlling costs and maintaining quality.
Looks at institutions that are majority-serving, tribal, Hispanic-serving, and
historically black. Emphasizes that the key to retention is in the professional
commitment of faculty and staff to student-centered efforts, and includes
practical ideas adaptable to different institutional goals.
ISBN: 0-7879-7974-0

IR124 **Unique Campus Contexts: Insights for Research and Assessment**
Jason E. Lane, M. Christopher Brown II
Summarizes what we know about professional schools, transnational campuses,
proprietary schools, religious institutions, and corporate universities. As more
students take advantage of these specialized educational environments,
conducting meaningful research becomes a challenge. The authors argue for the
importance of educational context and debunk the one-size-fits-all approach to
assessment, evaluation, and research. Effective institutional measures of
inquiry, benchmarks, and indicators must be congruent with the mission,
population, and function of each unique campus context.
ISBN: 0-7879-7973-2

IR123 **Successful Strategic Planning**
Michael J. Dooris, John M. Kelley, James F. Trainer
Explains the value of strategic planning in higher education to improve
conditions and meet missions (hiring better faculty, recruiting stronger
students, upgrading facilities, improving programs, acquiring resources), and
what planning tools and methodologies have been used at various campuses.
Goes beyond the activity of planning to investigate successful ways to implement
and infuse strategic plans throughout the organization. Case studies from
various campuses show different ways to achieve success.
ISBN: 0-7879-7792-6

IR122 **Assessing Character Outcomes in College**
Jon C. Dalton, Terrence R. Russell, Sally Kline
Examines several perspectives on the role of higher education in developing
students' character, and illustrates approaches to defining and assessing

character outcomes. Moral, civic, ethical, and spiritual development are key aspects of students' growth and experience in college, so how can educators encourage good values and assess their impact?
ISBN: 0-7879-7791-8

IR121   Overcoming Survey Research Problems
Stephen R. Porter
As demand for survey research has increased, survey response rates have decreased. This volume examines an array of survey research problems and best practices, from both the literature and field practitioners, to provide solutions to increase response rates while controlling costs. Discusses administering longitudinal studies, doing surveys on sensitive topics such as student drug and alcohol use, and using new technologies for survey administration.
ISBN: 0-7879-7477-3

IR120   Using Geographic Information Systems in Institutional Research
Daniel Teodorescu
Exploring the potential of geographic information systems (GIS) applications in higher education administration, this issue introduces IR professionals and campus administrators to a powerful presentation and analysis tool. Chapters explore the benefits of working with the spatial component of data in recruitment, admissions, facilities, alumni development, and other areas, with examples of actual GIS applications from several higher education institutions.
ISBN: 0-7879-7281-9

IR119   Maximizing Revenue in Higher Education
F. King Alexander, Ronald G. Ehrenberg
This volume presents edited versions of some of the best articles from a forum on institutional revenue generation sponsored by the Cornell Higher Education Research Institute. The chapters provide different perspectives on revenue generation and how institutions are struggling to find an appropriate balance between meeting public expectations and maximizing private market forces. The insights provided about options and alternatives will enable campus leaders, institutional researchers, and policymakers to better understand evolving patterns in public and private revenue reliance.
ISBN: 0-7879-7221-5

IR118   Studying Diverse Institutions: Contexts, Challenges, and Considerations
M. Christopher Brown II, Jason E. Lane
This volume examines the contextual and methodological issues pertaining to studying diverse institutions (including women's colleges, tribal colleges, and military academies), and provides effective and useful approaches for higher education administrators, institutional researchers and planners, policymakers, and faculty seeking to better understand students in postsecondary education. It also offers guidelines to asking the right research questions, employing the appropriate research design and methods, and analyzing the data with respect to the unique institutional contexts.
ISBN: 0-7879-6990-7

IR117   Unresolved Issues in Conducting Salary-Equity Studies
Robert K. Toutkoushian
Chapters discuss the issues surrounding how to use faculty rank, seniority, and experience as control variables in salary-equity studies. Contributors review the challenges of conducting a salary-equity study for nonfaculty administrators and staff—who constitute the majority of employees, even in academic institutions—and examine the advantages and disadvantages of using

hierarchical linear modeling to measure pay equity. They present a case-study approach to illustrate the political and practical challenges that researchers often face when conducting a salary-equity study for an institution. This is a companion volume to *Conducting Salary-Equity Studies: Alternative Approaches to Research* (IR115).
ISBN: 0-7879-6863-3

IR116   **Reporting Higher Education Results: Missing Links in the Performance Chain**
Joseph C. Burke, Henrick P. Minassians
The authors review performance reporting's coverage, content, and customers, they examine in depth the reporting indicators, types, and policy concerns, and they compare them among different states' reports. They highlight weaknesses in our current performance reporting—such as a lack of comparable indicators for assessing the quality of undergraduate education— and make recommendations about how to best use and improve performance information.
ISBN: 0-7879-6336-4

IR115   **Conducting Salary-Equity Studies: Alternative Approaches to Research**
Robert K. Toutkoushian
Synthesizing nearly 30 years of research on salary equity from the field of economics and the experiences of past studies, this issue launches an important dialogue between scholars and institutional researchers on the methodology and application of salary-equity studies in today's higher education institutions. The first of a two-volume set on the subject, it also bridges the gap between academic research and the more pragmatic statistical and political considerations in real-life institutional salary studies.
ISBN: 0-7879-6335-6

IR114   **Evaluating Faculty Performance**
Carol L. Colbeck
This issue brings new insights to faculty work and its assessment in light of reconsideration of faculty work roles, rapid technological change, increasing bureaucratization of the core work of higher education, and public accountability for performance. Exploring successful methods that individuals, institutions, and promotion and tenure committees are using for evaluations of faculty performance for career development, this issue is an indispensable guide to academic administrators and institutional researchers involved in the faculty evaluation process.
ISBN: 0-7879-6334-8

IR113   **Knowledge Management: Building a Competitive Advantage in Higher Education**
Andreea M. Serban, Jing Luan
Provides a comprehensive discussion of knowledge management, covering its theoretical, practical, and technological aspects with an emphasis on their relevance for applications in institutional research. Chapters examine the theoretical basis and impact of data mining; discuss the role of institutional research in customer relationship management; and provide a framework for the integration of institutional research within the larger context of organization learning. With a synopsis of technologies that support knowledge management and an exploration of future developments in this field, this volume assists institutional researchers and analysts in taking advantage of the opportunities of knowledge management and addressing its challenges.
ISBN: 0-7879-6291-0

NEW DIRECTIONS FOR INSTITUTIONAL RESEARCH

ORDER FORM SUBSCRIPTION AND SINGLE ISSUES

DISCOUNTED BACK ISSUES:

Use this form to receive 20% off all back issues of *New Directions for Institutional Research*.
All single issues priced at **$23.20** (normally $29.00)

TITLE	ISSUE NO.	ISBN
_____	_____	_____
_____	_____	_____
_____	_____	_____

*Call 888-378-2537 or see mailing instructions below. When calling, mention the promotional code JB9ND
to receive your discount. For a complete list of issues, please visit www.josseybass.com/go/ndir*

SUBSCRIPTIONS: (1 YEAR, 4 ISSUES)

☐ New Order   ☐ Renewal

U.S.	☐ Individual: $100	☐ Institutional: $249
CANADA/MEXICO	☐ Individual: $100	☐ Institutional: $289
ALL OTHERS	☐ Individual: $124	☐ Institutional: $323

*Call 888-378-2537 or see mailing and pricing instructions below.
Online subscriptions are available at www.interscience.wiley.com*

ORDER TOTALS:

Issue / Subscription Amount: $ _____

Shipping Amount: $ _____
(for single issues only – subscription prices include shipping)

Total Amount: $ _____

SHIPPING CHARGES:

First Item $5.00
Each Add'l Item $3.00

*(No sales tax for U.S. subscriptions. Canadian residents, add GST for subscription orders. Individual rate subscriptions must
be paid by personal check or credit card. Individual rate subscriptions may not be resold as library copies.)*

BILLING & SHIPPING INFORMATION:

☐ **PAYMENT ENCLOSED:** *(U.S. check or money order only. All payments must be in U.S. dollars.)*

☐ **CREDIT CARD:**   ☐ VISA   ☐ MC   ☐ AMEX

Card number _____ Exp. Date _____

Card Holder Name_____ Card Issue # _____

Signature _____ Day Phone _____

☐ **BILL ME:** *(U.S. institutional orders only. Purchase order required.)*

Purchase order # _____
              Federal Tax ID 13559302 • GST 89102-8052

Name_____

Address_____

Phone_____ E-mail_____

Copy or detach page and send to: **John Wiley & Sons, PTSC, 5th Floor
                                        989 Market Street, San Francisco, CA 94103-1741**

Order Form can also be faxed to: **888-481-2665**

PROMO JB9ND

Get Online Access to
New Directions for Institutional Research

New Directions for Institutional Research is available through Wiley InterScience, the dynamic online content service from John Wiley & Sons. Visit our Web site and enjoy a range of extremely useful features:

WILEY INTERSCIENCE ALERTS
  Content Alerts: Receive tables of contents alerts via e-mail as soon as a new issue is online.
  Profiled Alerts: Set up your own e-mail alerts based on personal queries, keywords, and other parameters.

QUICK AND POWERFUL SEARCHING
  Browse and Search functions are designed to lead you to the information you need quickly and easily. Whether searching by title, keyword, or author, your results will point directly to the journal article, book chapter, encyclopedia entry or database you seek.

PERSONAL HOME PAGE
  Store and manage Wiley InterScience Alerts, searches, and links to key journals and articles.

MOBILEEDITION™
  Download table of contents and abstracts to your PDA every time you synchronize.

CROSSREF®
  Move seamlessly from a reference in a journal article to the cited journal articles, which may be located on a different server and published by a different publisher.

LINKS
  Navigate to and from indexing and abstracting services.

For more information about online access, please contact us at: North, Central, and South America: 1-800-511-3989, uscs-wis@wiley.com
All other regions: (+44) (0) 1243-843-345, cs-wis@wiley.co.uk

www.interscience.wiley.com

Statement of Ownership, Management, and Circulation
(All Periodicals Publications Except Requester Publications)

1. Publication Title	2. Publication Number	3. Filing Date
New Directions for Institutional Research	0 2 7 1 _ 0 5 7 9	10/1/2008

4. Issue Frequency	5. Number of Issues Published Annually	6. Annual Subscription Price
Quarterly	4	$230

7. Complete Mailing Address of Known Office of Publication (Not printer) (Street, city, county, state, and ZIP+4®)	Contact Person
Wiley Subscriptions Services, Inc. at Jossey-Bass, 989 Market St., San Francisco, CA 94103	Joe Schuman
	Telephone (Include area code) 415-782-3232

8. Complete Mailing Address of Headquarters or General Business Office of Publisher (Not printer)

Wiley Subscriptions Services, Inc., 111 River Street, Hoboken, NJ 07030

9. Full Names and Complete Mailing Addresses of Publisher, Editor, and Managing Editor (Do not leave blank)

Publisher (Name and complete mailing address)

Wiley Subscriptions Services, Inc., A Wiley Company at San Francisco, 989 Market St., San Francisco, CA 94103-1741

Editor (Name and complete mailing address)

Robert Toutkoushian, Educational Leadership/ Policy Studies Education 4220, Indiana Univ., Bloomington IN 47405

Managing Editor (Name and complete mailing address)

Robert Rosenberg, Wiley Subscriptions Services, Inc., 989 Market Street, San Francisco, CA 94103

10. Owner (Do not leave blank. If the publication is owned by a corporation, give the name and address of the corporation immediately followed by the names and addresses of all stockholders owning or holding 1 percent or more of the total amount of stock. If not owned by a corporation, give the names and addresses of the individual owners. If owned by a partnership or other unincorporated firm, give its name and address as well as those of each individual owner. If the publication is published by a nonprofit organization, give its name and address.)

Full Name	Complete Mailing Address
Wiley Subscriptions Services	111 River Street, Hoboken, NJ
(see attached list)	

11. Known Bondholders, Mortgagees, and Other Security Holders Owning or Holding 1 Percent or More of Total Amount of Bonds, Mortgages, or Other Securities. If none, check box ➤ ☑ None

Full Name	Complete Mailing Address

12. Tax Status (For completion by nonprofit organizations authorized to mail at nonprofit rates) (Check one)
The purpose, function, and nonprofit status of this organization and the exempt status for federal income tax purposes:
☐ Has Not Changed During Preceding 12 Months
☐ Has Changed During Preceding 12 Months (Publisher must submit explanation of change with this statement)

13. Publication Title	14. Issue Date for Circulation Data
New Directions for Institutional Research	Summer 2008

15. Extent and Nature of Circulation			Average No. Copies Each Issue During Preceding 12 Months	No. Copies of Single Issue Published Nearest to Filing Date
a. Total Number of Copies (Net press run)			1549	1357
b. Paid Circulation (By Mail and Outside the Mail)	(1)	Mailed Outside-County Paid Subscriptions Stated on PS Form 3541 (Include paid distribution above nominal rate, advertiser's proof copies, and exchange copies)	629	480
	(2)	Mailed In-County Paid Subscriptions Stated on PS Form 3541 (Include paid distribution above nominal rate, advertiser's proof copies, and exchange copies)	0	0
	(3)	Paid Distribution Outside the Mails Including Sales Through Dealers and Carriers, Street Vendors, Counter Sales, and Other Paid Distribution Outside USPS®	0	0
	(4)	Paid Distribution by Other Classes of Mail Through the USPS (e.g. First-Class Mail®)	0	0
c. Total Paid Distribution (Sum of 15b (1), (2),(3), and (4))			629	480
d. Free or Nominal Rate Distribution (By Mail and Outside the Mail)	(1)	Free or Nominal Rate Outside-County Copies Iincluded on PS Form 3541	49	51
	(2)	Free or Nominal Rate In-County Copies Included on PS Form 3541	0	0
	(3)	Free or Nominal Rate Copies Mailed at Other Classes Through the USPS (e.g. First-Class Mail)	0	0
	(4)	Free or Nominal Rate Distribution Outside the Mail (Carriers or other means)	0	0
e. Total Free or Nominal Rate Distribution (Sum of 15d (1), (2), (3) and (4)			49	51
f. Total Distribution (Sum of 15c and 15e)		➤	678	531
g. Copies not Distributed (See Instructions to Publishers #4 (page #3))		➤	871	826
h. Total (Sum of 15f and g)		➤	1549	1357
i. Percent Paid (15c divided by 15f times 100)		➤	93%	90%

16. Publication of Statement of Ownership

☐ If the publication is a general publication, publication of this statement is required. Will be printed in the ___Winter 2008___ issue of this publication.

☐ Publication not required.

17. Signature and Title of Editor, Publisher, Business Manager, or Owner	Date
Susan E. Lewis, VP & Publisher - Periodicals *(signature)*	10/1/2008

I certify that all information furnished on this form is true and complete. I understand that anyone who furnishes false or misleading information on this form or who omits material or information requested on the form may be subject to criminal sanctions (including fines and imprisonment) and/or civil sanctions (including civil penalties).